THE CASTLE ON
GIBBET HILL

THE CASTLE ON GIBBET HILL

THE SURPRISING HISTORY OF GROTON, MASSACHUSETTS

BY CHERIE DUMONT

DEDICATED TO MY CHILDREN:
SAGE AND NILE

Published in 2023 by Salmon of Knowledge Books, Whitefish, Montana
Library of Congress Control Number: 2023909210
ISBN 979-8-9878805-0-0
eISBN e979-8-9878805-1-7

Design by Peppis Designworks

CONTENTS

THE LAY OF THE LAND

HIGH GROUND

Long before the Massachusetts Bay Colony established itself in the wildlands of the New World, the indigenous people who hunted and gathered the area that later would be named Groton, used high ground. Central Massachusetts was thickly forested, dotted with lakes.

Traveling on foot, as they had to, was tough going in the summer months when the woods were thick with vines, briars, and undergrowth. They made heavy use of animal paths, but seeing beyond a few yards was nearly impossible. So the native people climbed up to the places that allowed them to see a wider area. From the highest point, known today as Gibbet Hill (elevation: 469 feet), they might have been able to see the ocean. Visibility is commonly estimated to be 60 to 70 miles, which "makes the white mountains seem like neighbors". Bonfires, which were then a means of communication, can be spotted more than 30 miles to the west and east.

Throughout the pre-colonial period, a large swamp to Gibbet Hill's west and a pond to the north had open tillable meadows. What was ultimately named Martin's Pond was much bigger than it is today, and it emptied into a much larger James Brook by way of Half Moon Meadow at the base of Gibbet Hill. To the southwest is Mount Wachusett (elevation: 2,006 feet). To the northwest is the smaller Mount Watatuck (elevation: 1,831 feet). To the east stretch the great plains leading to the Atlantic Ocean.

The large swamp at the base of Gibbet Hill has evidence of glacial activity in the past. New England was covered in ice 10,000 years ago. As the ice sheet began to thin and slow, it left behind many small mounds of gravel and sand. Gibbet Hill is rounded at its top but elongated on the north–south axis, the direction of glacial movement, making it a good example of a large drumlin. The ice sheet also churned up plenty of boulders.

In 1900, Italian stonemasons used those boulders to build what we now know as the castle on Gibbet Hill.

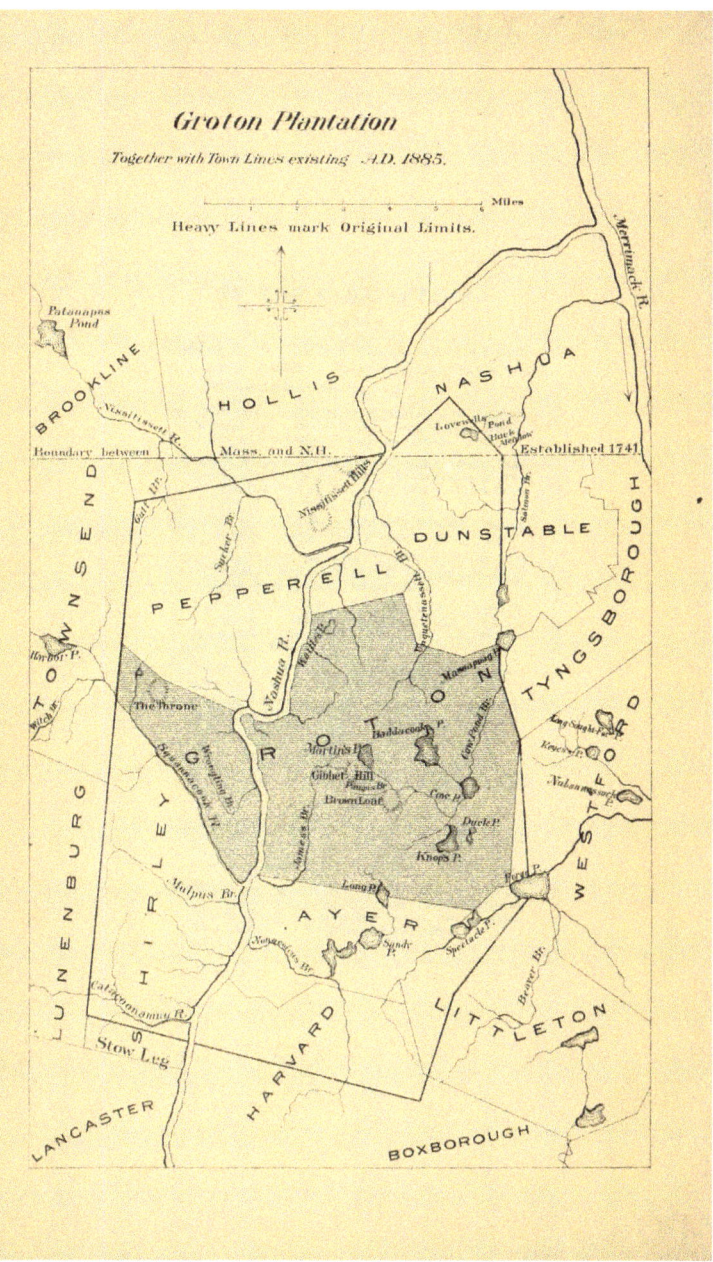

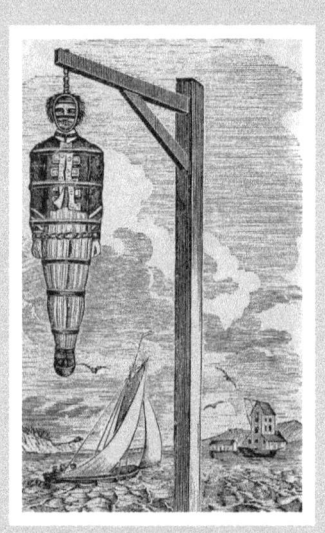

CHAPTER ONE

TAKE NOTE OF GIBBET HILL

THE LEGEND

Gibbet Hill "shoulders and carries the most thrilling, romantic, and blood-curdling story in the town's rich history," writes John Keep Nutting in 1908. "Only a decade since, I heard this story related by a very aged resident, with evident faith in it as genuine history." Legends often have a kernel of truth. Mr. Nutting's story is quoted here word for word.

> *Once upon a time, as this story goes, a Dreadful Pirate was caught in Groton. Some say that he had wandered so far inland in order to hide the more securely a great pot of doubloons, his share of the proceeds of many a bloody capture on the high seas. Some say he was one of Captain Kidd's men. Anyhow, he was caught, and of his guilt there was no doubt. So they set up a tall gibbet upon that high hill, in sight of the town, and there the wretch was hung. But not by his neck. Oh no. That would be too good for him. He was HUNG-IN-CHAINS! And there he was left to swing in the wind, until slow starvation, or the torture of the chains, should end his cursed existence! And to deal with him somewhat more in accordance with his desserts, a loaf of bread was so suspended that as it also swung in the wind, it would ever and anon strike against his famished lips, while the vile wretch could not get a morsel of it!*
>
> *Strange to say, that Critical Spirit of our times, which forbids William Tell to be taken seriously, and which has chopped George Washington's cherry-tree all to pieces, has dared to meddle with this story of Gibbet hill. It has been held that no such event ever took place. The whole thing was a half-remembered night-mare story, brought over by some foolish pioneer, and loaded bodily upon our poor innocent Gibbet hill because it stood convenient. Some such horror may have been enacted in old England, but in America—never!*

All the same, I hold fast to the story of Gibbet hill. Criticism may be high, but Gibbet hill rises above it. For how could any one have managed to win a first believer for that story, if nothing of the kind had ever happened? And how can any one explain the undeniable fact that practically all the old residents of Groton truly believed the story, and handed it down from generation to generation, with all its gruesome particulars, on the supposition that those who set the story going, knew that it had no foundation?

Besides, I myself have heard the horrible shrieks and groans of the poor Pirate, and the creaking and clanking of his chains—of a pitch-dark, boisterous March night! The hill is a mile from the Village, yet I have heard the shrieks and groans from a still greater distance—and have taken to my heels in sore fright. And how could a small boy have heard the shrieks, if there had never been any Pirate to shriek?

Many Gibbet Hills

Whatever the truth of the pirate story, we know that Groton's first town clerk, Richard Sawtell, entered Gibbet Hill into the public record on June 23, 1662, as being part of the land grant of Sergeant James Parker. Groton's early historian, Dr. Samuel Green, tells a story of a Native American being gibbeted on the hill, though Isabel Beal, Groton's historian of the late 20th century, did not believe it. She thought the English settlers were reminded of a Gibbet Hill in the old country.

Gibbet Hill is not a unique place name. References can be found as far back as 1225. In North America, St. John's, Newfoundland, has a Gibbet Hill. Ellis Island also has Gibbet Hill. One web site, called the "Mystery Tour of Britain," talks about one on Beacon Edge near Penrith in Cumbria, England with a resident ghost named Nicholson. Mr. Nicholson murdered his godfather, Thomas Parker, and was convicted, hung, and then placed in an iron cage hanging on the main road. His uneasy spirit is still said to be seen today by local residents as a skeletal apparition trapped in his gibbet.

Another Gibbet Hill, in Hindhead Commons, 12 miles southwest of Guildford, was the last stop for many a highwayman. Rising 894 feet, this sandstone hill is now part of a National Trust complex.

A series of five paintings produced by a Hindhead innkeeper named Pearson depicting the event leading up to the murder were used to illustrate an anonymous poem about the murder of the Unknown Sailor as he is called. Before World War I, four of the paintings were commemorated in postcards. The paintings, originally hung in the Royal Huts Hotel, Hindhead, Surrey, were moved to the banqueting room of The Kings Arms, Godalming, Surrey and were lost until they were bought at auction and retired to the Haslemere Museum. Perhaps the most famous Gibbet Hill in Britain is the one on the Kenilworth Road out of Coventry. Coventry has a well-known university and is where Jaguar motorcars are still manufactured. The Benedictine Abbey was established in 1043 by Leofric, Earl of Mercia and his wife, Lady Godiva. The scaffold was once located at the crossroad on the crest of the hill. The intersection is now on the campus of the Warwick Medical School and is the scene of numerous auto accidents.

Punishment in the Colonies

A 17th century gibbeting added to the atmosphere of a market day where people could buy summer vegetables, hammered pots, animals squawking in wooden cages, and leather goods. The entire village would be wearing their best clothing. An execution was a common occurance to the market-goers who were used to death.

By 12 years old, most children had seen a sibling die of smallpox after an agonizing day of writhing. It was their job to kill chickens for the stew pot. When a family's only horse fell and snapped a leg, a child might hold the halter while it was put down. Death, like the sun and rain, was always present and could come at any moment.

Colonials came to the market on gibbeting day to see justice done. In a world filled with events they could not control, the black-clothed ministers explained that to cull the sick, punish the wicked, and call the virtuous home was God's will.

Settlers came to the shores of New England to form societies pleasing in God's eyes. Through his agents of the Church, a displeased deity had the divine right to take terrible retribution for disobedience. English planters felt they were chosen by God to bring order to the evil nature of Man. And Man's true nature was base and wild and must be resisted and disciplined. Exposing an average sinner to the judgment of the gibbet gave others a chance to contemplate the error of their ways.

Severe pain was an appropriate punishment for a crime against God. Suffering got at the source of the crime—the evil body. A guilty body part was often severed from the sinner in hopes that the remainder might live a better life. Crimes could be extremely slight by modern standards. In 18th century England, for example, a sentence for blasphemy meant you would never speak again. A counterfeiter lost one hand. Gossipy women had their fiery tongues cooled by dunking in ice-cold water. Corporal or capital punishment was considered educational. The feudal lords of Europe carried this idea to the New World.

The death penalty had been around for a very long time. It is recorded in the ancient laws of China, and in the 18th century BC, the Babylonians had 25 different crimes in their Code of King Hammurabi that would end in death if you were caught—although, strangely enough, murder was not one of these. The Egyptians in the 16th century BC were the first civilization to enter a sentence of death into the public record. A nobleman accused of unlawful magic was given the opportunity to take his own life. A common stone worker was beheaded with an ax. By the 10th century, hanging was the most popular method.

In New England, in 1608 George Kendall of Virginia was

executed for allegedly plotting to betray the British to the Spanish. In 1612, one could be put to death in Virginia for stealing grapes, killing chickens (presumably other people's chickens, rather than their own), killing dogs or horses without permission, or trading with Indians. Seven years later these laws were softened, perhaps because it was feared settlers would leave and take up clearing land in a more reasonable colony.

Massachusetts put its first criminal to death in 1630. In 1636, the death penalty could be handed down for premeditated murder, sodomy, witchcraft (à la Salem), adultery, idolatry, blasphemy, rape, and eight other crimes. By 1780, the Commonwealth was down to seven: murder, sodomy, burglary, buggery, arson, rape, and treason.

The Gibbet

According to a 1727 encyclopedia, a "gibet" is a "machine in manner of a gallows, whereon notorious criminals after execution, are hung in irons, or chains, as spectacles, in terrorism." It's interesting that the word "gibet" has derivations that cover both its projecting arm, neck rope, and metal cage, for the old French "gibe" was a sort of sickle or hook; the old English is also "jib", as in a type of sail; and the Italian version "gibba" is an under waistcoat or doublet.

A standard gallows would kill a criminal, but after a few weeks crows and gravity would return the remains to the dignity of the earth. By contrast, a gibbet would display the dead body of a criminal, swinging in the wind for days, weeks, and even years. Ingeniously designed, gibbets held a corpse together in a recognizable human shape almost indefinitely.

The earliest hanging cages were suspended from city walls, palaces and even cathedrals. Often the victim was still very much alive when they were locked in the cage. Naked or nearly naked, they were left to the elements and succumbed to thirst, hunger, or the winter cold or summer heat. Rows of gibbets were often installed at the major crossroads of a town and remained swaying for years.

Death by Hanging

People who have seen American Western movies believe hanging is an instant death by broken neck. However, the majority of documented hanging victims did not sustain a neck fracture or even a spinal injury. Instead, the gallows subjects the victim to a host of indignities before strangulation causes death. Beheading is humane compared with hanging.

After the push, the rope dislocates the neck, which, of course, is extremely painful. The now-taut rope abrades and stretches the skin on the neck. It obstructs the jugular vein but not the ascending aorta which is residing in the deeper tissue, this means blood continues to be pumped into the head under high pressure but cannot get out, so the head begins to bulge out like a cantaloupe-sized aneurysm. The eyes pop and the tongue swells. The pressure inside the skull builds and builds, giving the victim the mother of all migraines.

The rope also obstructs the windpipe, sometimes crushing it, so the carbon dioxide level in the blood rises, causing a reflexive urge to inhale, which becomes a full-blown panic as the body tries to stop the strangulation by alerting all systems to FIND AIR NOW. The body will jerk and twist as it tries to free its windpipe and the person will desperately try to cry for help; but of course there is no sound because no air can flow over the vocal cords. No inhalation means a drop in oxygen saturation in the blood, which stimulates the autonomic nervous system to release fluids from every possible exit. Out flow the sweat, saliva, urine, and feces. Finally the person will lose consciousness when their oxygen levels and blood pressure drop enough, and the excruciating pain will blessedly be over—but that is not the end of it. They are still alive. It is truly amazing to contemplate just how much it takes to kill a person.

Next, one of two things used to happen. First scenario: After half an hour or so, the victim would be cut down and carried to a block, where a hooded executioner equipped with a specially designed ax partially severed the neck. Their assistant hacked off the rest with a butcher knife. The separated head was grabbed by its blood-soaked hair and held up for all to see with a cry, which typically went, "Behold the head of a [traitor, murderer, adulterer, etc.]."

Second Scenario: The victim would be cut down after a much longer period, to ensure death had occurred.

In both cases, the body would then be placed in a cage of iron bands in the shape of a human being, encircling the torso, head, and limbs. On its top hung a ring with a chain attached and the chain was hooked back up to a wooden arm, where it remained for months or even years.

For example, in Stoneleigh, England three convicted murderers—Moses Baker, Edward Drury, and Robert Leslie—were put in a cart in 1765 and hauled to the common. The records of the day report the men "behaved in a decent manner, acknowledged the justice of their sentence, freely forgave everyone who had been instrumental in convicting them and said they were sorry for their behavior at their trial" (they had threatened to blow the out the brains in Alderman Hewitt's head). The men shook hands, kissed each other on the cheek, and climbed up the platform to their nooses.

The ladders were pulled out and the men kicked and twitched until dead. The bodies received a tar coating to hold them together and were placed in a "close fitted harness" of chain and steel. The corpses were then re-hung on the gib.

The Halifax Gibbet

The people of Halifax, England, found a much more efficient way to execute. They combined the messy decapitation and subsequent display in one easy machine. The town had conducted executions since 1066 but it was in 1286 that it gained the notoriety by which it still draws tourists to this day. John of Dalton had the distinction of being the first to be decapitated by the Halifax Gibbet.

The Halifax Gibbet eliminated the axeman and the butcher knife. Instead, a transverse beam fixed with a sliding block with an ax attached and a weight of seven pounds twelve ounces was used. The ax was drawn up the grooves of the side timbers by a cord and pulley. Daniel Defoe's account of Halifax in his work *A Tour through the Whole Island of Great Britain* (1724–1727) assures us of the effectiveness of the engine. The force was "so strong, the head of the ax being loaded with a weight of lead to make it fall heavy, and the execution so secure, that it takes away the possibility of its failing to cut off the head."

This particular invention came about partly because of a cottage industry. Newly manufactured cloth was delivered to the town weekly, cleaned in an abundance of spring water, and laid out to dry on wooden tenter frames, covering the local hillsides with billowing bright fabric. The bolts of cloth were a temptation for thefts and gave rise to the need for a gibbet on the hill for Saturdays, the day of the main market. As chef Thomas Keller says: "Any job worth doing, is worth doing well. But to be able to do that, you have to do it over and over again."

Gibbet Hill   From the Original picture at the "Royal Huts" Hotel, Hindhead.

Placed in chains, and there close by   Hanging there both night and day,
The London Road to be hung on high,   And on the spot where the foul deed was done,
Where travellers by coach or van   Till piece by piece they dropped away;
All hear the tale of the murdered man,   Can now be seen by everyone;
As they near the gibbet tree–   And on that spot the travellers know,
A sight more loathsome none could see.   No heath nor grass doth ever grow.

ABOVE: Postcard #4 in Unknown Sailor murder collection circa1920 (Frith series, Surrey).

BELOW LEFT: A new method of macarony making, as practiced at Boston (British Cartoon Prints Collection, Library of Congress, print published in London in 1774).

BELOW RIGHT: The body of Captain Kidd (Wood engraving by George Hodder, Liverpool, 1810).

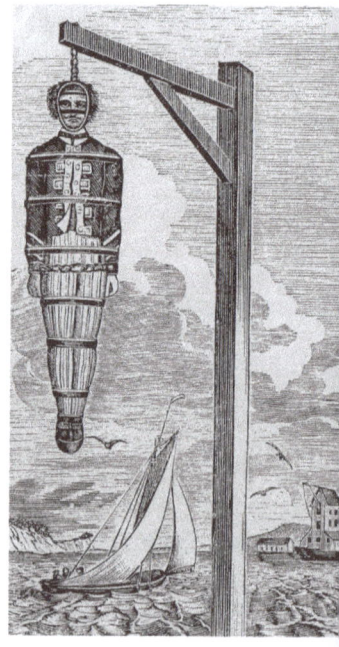

CHAPTER 2

GROTON PLANTATION

THE ALGONQUIN

The first peoples of Groton were most likely the Nipmuc (meaning literally "small pond" or "freshwater place") and bands of the Pennacook ("at the bottom of the hill", also known as the Merrimac). The land around Groton was a borderland between the two groups. Almost all of the people of the East Coast spoke languages related to the Eastern Algonquin family, from Nova Scotia to North Carolina. The further one got from the home territory the harder it was to understand, though there was probably still enough in common to trade some fish or game.

The main encampment near Groton was called Nashaway or "place between waters", along the present Nashua River near West Groton and Shirley and south to Lancaster. The leader of this group was the notorious Sagamore Sam who joined forces with King Philip in 1675 and began a campaign to burn all the European settlements within his territory. Another smaller band had its village on the west banks of the Nashua along what is now Route 119 in Pepperell.

The Nipmuc

Most of the Algonquin peoples of the East Coast were agricultural as well as hunter-gatherers. The Nipmucs acquired 65–85% of their daily requirements from agriculture and formed villages during the spring and summer, mostly along the rivers or on the large ponds, both of which are abundant in Groton. They changed camps according to the season, but remained within their territories. Several times during the year a great encampment of related Nipmucs enjoyed the ancestral homeland near Brookfield, Massachusetts, or Washacum in present-day Sterling. Though they did not live as well as their coastal cousins, food was not scarce, and they planted corn, beans, and squash around the fertile river floodplains and beaver ponds. Some of the growing fields were extensive, several hundred acres in cultivation. During the winter, the people receded into the now navigable forests and broke up into smaller bands of a few wigwams. Hunting and tracking was easier and was supplemented with corn that had been dried and stored.

There was never a Nipmuc Tribe. Nipmuc is a geographical classification given to the people who lived in central Massachusetts and southern New Hampshire. Each kin group was ruled by its own sachem. They lived in independent bands which at different times were allied to, or subject to, powerful native warlords surrounding them. The villages of Massomuck, Monashackotook, and Quinnebaug, on the south and west borderlands, were Nipmuc, but they were subject to the Pequot (a sub-branch of the Mohegans) before the Pequot were destroyed by the English.

The Nashaway, a group of Algonquins in Lancaster and probably Groton, were at one time subject to the Pennacook and Sokoni to the north and northwest of traditional lands. Whereas the majority of Pennacook, Wampanoags, and Pequots lived in fortified compounds, the Nipmuc did not, so what little warfare was around must have been manageable. These people seemed to be more at peace with each other and their neighboring bands.

The Greatest Killer in History

Before contact with white traders, the Pennacook numbered about 12,000 in 30 villages. The Nipmuc, whose range extended over the central plateau of Massachusetts into northern Rhode Island and northeastern Connecticut, numbered as many as 10,000 in 40 villages. But from 1564, their numbers plummeted.

The first recorded outbreak of smallpox came to America either from Canada or the West Indies in 1616–19. Trying its best to infect all humans, smallpox continued to return, destroying villages in 1649, 1670, 1677, 1679, 1687, 1691, 1729, 1733, 1755, and 1758. In between those dates, influenza and diphtheria came to call. By 1750, the population of native people had been reduced to a few thousand where once there had been over 30,000.

It is hard to imagine how terrifying this must have been.

One day a family member would develop a fever, then a rash, and in two weeks everyone in the village would be sick. In Europe, the fatality rate was normally an appalling 20–60%, but in the previously unexposed native population the fatality rate was very close to 100%. The incidence rate was so high that without a vaccine everyone would eventually get smallpox.

Thomas Morton, a lawyer and trader, lived among the Algonquin near Quincy, MA. His account of the Native Americans is the opposite of that of Puritan William Bradford. He credits the Native Americans with personal modesty, hospitality for strangers, respect for authority, and closeness to nature in a way that almost mirrors the revisionist history of the late 20th century. He's an interesting read. In his Manners and Customs of the Indians, 1637, he writes about the smallpox epidemic:"...they died in heaps as they lay in their houses; and the living, that were able to shift themselves, would run away and let them die, and let their carcasses lie above the ground without burial, for in a place where many inhabited, there had been but one left to live to tell what became of the rest; the living being (as it seems) not able to bury the dead, they are left for crows, kites, and vermin to prey upon."

John Winthrop, founder of the Massachusetts Bay Colony, announced that "God hath consumed the natives with a miraculous plague, whereby, the greater part of the country is left void of inhabitants." The land was now free for occupation. In the early records of Charlestown, the townspeople felt "by which awful and admirable dispensation it pleased God to make room for his people of the English nation; who after this...without this remarkable and terrible stroke of God upon the natives, would with much more difficulty have found room, and at a far greater charge have obtained and purchased land."

The English did not move into wild, tangled forestland. There were open fields that had been kept fertile for generations by loving native husbandry. Clever Nipmucs burned the underbrush to improve soil condition and to keep it cleared of scrub. Clearing virgin forest for crops was a grueling job and the English were only too happy to move into improved land.

Unwilling to engage in open warfare with the British, the Nipmuc began to sell off parts of their lands. In the Lancaster Purchase (1643); the Tantisuque Deed (1644); and the Eliot and Brookfield Purchases (1655), the best farmlands in the river valleys went to the buyers. The Nipmuc did not understand what they had done. Nipmuc scholar Dennis Connole writes, "Originally, the Indian sachem deeded his land to the English in exchange for protection for himself and his people. The Indian believed the land would be used in common and most deeds reserved the right to hunt, fish, plant at convenient locations, set their wigwams, and use the woodland trees for firewood. It appears that in some cases the English were well aware of the Indian intent to share the land without giving clear title; in numerous cases they paid for the same piece of land two or more times. Upon the death of a ruling sachem, the English would obtain confirmation of an existing deed from the succeeding party with payments in money and goods. Under this agreement the sachems were willing to allow the English access to large tracts of land and in some instances their entire domain."

To the Algonquin, land was unownable. It was a fluid resource used by specific people with traditional rights. It could be won back in warfare or through the settling of a debt, or because the current occupants moved to another tract. While the Nipmuc realized the superior power of the English and knew they must compromise, it was unimaginable to them that the English would force them forever from their homelands. At first their trust was well placed. The Puritan missionaries gave them protection and food and formed them into "praying villages" of Christian converts. From time to time, groups would break up and re-form if conflicts persisted but they were used to governing themselves and if it pleased them to follow the Christian god for a spell, they did just that, but when the sachem

Metacomet called the native peoples into a grand confederation to fight the English colonists during King Philip's War, the Nipmucs of the praying villages joined up.

The English Colony

Groton was the first American frontier. It was also the birthplace of the expansive American consciousness of today. People came here from across the Atlantic knowing that beyond the trading post was free land, room to make a new start, room to disappear, room to fail—until all this officially ended in 1890 with a bulletin from the superintendent of the census stating "there can hardly be said to be a frontier line...westward movement, etc., it can not, therefore, any longer have a place in the census reports."

The first men came to Groton on the invitation of King Charles I, who owned New England and it was (from the English perspective) his to grant or not to grant as he saw fit. He had inherited it from his father, King James, the successor to Elizabeth I. But an entire continent was burning a hole in his pocket, so he granted much of it to Sir Henry Roswell in the third year of his reign. The tracts were measured by river boundaries, the Massachuset River (which became the Charles) and the Merrimack "from sea to sea." Calling this land Plymouth, Henry Roswell with five others, and 14 associates incorporated it as the "Governor and Company of the Massachusetts Bay in New England." Forty-four towns were established within Plymouth and Massachusetts colonies before 1653.

The next year, Deane Winthrop, son of Governor John Winthrop who had celebrated the decimation of the natives, joined with several others to petition his father for a plantation all his own, to be called "Groaten." One of the men, John Tinker, probably was a squatter before he joined in the petition, trading for years with the Nashaway bands. One of his trading posts was at the natural ford where another creek flowed into the Nashua. That little stream became known as Nod Creek (the land of Nod). The Indians called the place Petapawag.

Shells as Currency

In 1657, John Tinker paid £8 for the "privilege of trafficking with these Indians at Groton and Lancaster MA." Eight pounds was a very stiff business permit rate, being the equivalent of $1,150 today. Tinker traded for furred animal skins that were all the rage in Europe. He must have used wampum shell beads in exchange, which had been declared legal tender in 1637, valued at six beads a penny (60 cents today). The beads were painstakingly fashioned into two types—white ones, sliced from the inner whorls of a periwinkle, and a double-valued purple or black bead cut out of the dark segments of the quahog or hard-shelled clam. Before the Europeans started to mass-produce them, shells were gathered during the summer by the native people of Long Island Sound, and crafted during the winter months, requiring tedious grinding and polishing of the shells into tubes approximately 6.7 mm long by 4.7 mm in diameter with the center drilled by means of an invention called a puckwhegonnautick. The beads would be sewn into belts, aprons, capes, earrings, headpieces, necklaces, and other items strung with fibers of hemp or the tendons of deer. The Nipmuc traded furs and food for the precious strings of beads.

Wampum was certainly used in simple exchange for goods, but also embodied an ethic of gift-giving. It could be used as a trophy, bribe, restitution, marriage proposal, and even compensation for a murdered family member. The Puritan aversion to assassination was considered prudish by Algonquins. Only persons of high rank and their families could get away with wearing their money.

Reciprocity among tribes helped to keep the peace and elaborate rituals were followed to prevent a breakdown in social equilibrium. Unlike the West Coast tribes' practice of potlatch, where the leaders of a band gave away everything to maintain their status, sachems and other officials were paid tribute by their villages affording them a lavish lifestyle, but wisely, the sachems redistributed the wampum in ceremonies, rituals, and games. Intriguingly, wampum was also used for communication and as a memory device. Designs woven into belts recorded trades and important events, and even became accounts books. A person would be designated "keeper of the belt". The black bead signified war or mourning, the white bead symbolized peace, and when a belt bore bad news, it was publicly kicked around.

New England Frontier Towns

By 1656, Groton was granted township status and set about attracting men to build a town. John Tinker lived in Groton and Lancaster but most of the original grantees did not. These men were speculators but few engaged in the ungentlemanly tasks of clearing trees and stacking the stones heaved up each winter. Deane Winthrop, for example, stayed in Boston where he could get a newspaper and stay fairly clean.

Farmers need neighbors to help with the haying or give rescue to a cow in a jam. By 1659, John Tinker had become disgusted by the absence of inhabitants and sent a petition to the General Court in Boston asking for the help he needed to survive on the frontier. The court responded by sending three men to check out the situation. They found only six families actually living there even though there was room for 60. The speculators were holding onto land and, in some cases, fudging the total number of acres in their holdings. The court heard rumors that the Indians were starting to understand what the English had meant when they 'bought' the land. The committee doled out 50 acres each to the six families, and divided the rest to accommodate at least 60 other families. If the absent grantee didn't occupy their lands within two years, they would not only forfeit the grant but also be charged 20 shillings per acre.

Groton was not the only town with this problem. In 1694, the

General Court of Massachusetts enumerated an act to support the "Frontier towns...which the inhabitants were forbidden to desert on pain of loss of their lands (if landowners) or of imprisonment (if not landowners), unless permission to remove were first obtained." The frontier towns were Wells, York, and Kittery, Maine (part of Massachusetts) and Amesbury, Haverhill, Dunstable, Chelmsford, Groton, Lancaster, Marlborough, and Deerfield, MA.

The way the colonists set up their frontier towns is fascinating. Each town was owned by the grantees as "tenants in common." This didn't mean they owned equal proportions. Groton began as a square 8 by 8 miles (i.e. 64 square miles; 40,960 acres). In a first stab at zoning, the grantees parceled the land into 755 parts called "acre rights". A man granted a 60-acre right, would have been entitled to 3,242 acres. No one man was to be granted a majority of acre rights. In the first booking of names set down in 1716, 50 men held acres rights; the average holding was 14 acre rights. Richard Blood held 60, Captain James Parker, the most prominent man in town, held 50 (which included Gibbet Hill) and Senator William Longely had 30. The rest had 20 or less, with the least being five.

An acre right entitled a man to one vote in a town meeting. Some land held in common was doled out for use according to a man's acre rights. Every grantee had use of some upland and every man had meadow. They built their houses next to other houses in town, the better to protect them from attack. This joint decision-making about the use of the town as an entirety ensured that all the cows could be fed and all the houses could be defended. No one had all the good meadow or all the rocky intervale. Everyone had access to good water, although this is not difficult in Groton. The planters made hay together on communal land.

Eventually, land in common began to be sold off to pay for the meeting house and other public buildings. Conflicts did crop up, of course. People complained that the fields were not equal or not of the same size and committees were set up to address these problems. Groton still has a remnant of this—a volunteer in the present town government settles disputes about the location and condition of fences.

In the beginning, one acre right entitled you to the use of 54 acres of land. As time went on, the amount of acres which constituted an "acre right" began to shrink as commonly held land was sold off to generate revenue. By 1727 it was down to six acres and, by the last division, one-quarter acre of the best land and three acres of the poorest land. The original proprietors of Groton and their descendants continued to divide up common plots until 1829.

The residents of Groton had lived in relative peace with the Algonquin living west of the Nashua River for 15 years after the town was established. Then Metacomet, a Wampanoag sachem, used his formidable organizational skills to band together all the Algonquin tribes to stop the takeover of ancestral lands. King Philip's War officially began in late June 1675 when a settler near Swansea killed a Wampanoag Indian. In retaliation the Wampanoags attacked Swansea and killed eight.

The Burning of Groton

The winter of 1675–76 was cold. Major Simon Willard of Lancaster maintained a scouting party of 40 troopers and dragoons to patrol the territory between Marlborough and Groton. Major Willard's son, Samuel, petitioned the General Council at Cambridge expressing concerns about the safety of the families residing in frontier towns. Twenty soldiers were dispatched to guard the garrison houses.

On the night of March 2, 1676, Nipmuc warriors under Sagamore Sam came into Groton and shot into eight or nine houses. They stole some cattle and faded back into the trees. The alarmed families drove their cattle into the meadow in the shadow of Gibbet Hill and transferred stores of food into the five garrison houses in the center of town. The Nipmucs then began to terrorize the farmers. Some warriors stole into town and overturned three outbuildings and confiscated corn, pigs, and chickens and then proceeded to cook and eat them in front of the townspeople. Two days later four villagers built up enough courage to grab a cart and try to fill it with hay for their animals. They were ambushed. Two of them got away but one was killed and the other captured. The dead man was stripped naked, hacked up, and laid on his back in the road as a warning. The other man escaped and ran all the way to the garrison in Lancaster.

On the morning of March 13, the townspeople were feeling more relaxed. A patrol had been sent out the day before without finding any Nipmuc in the area. That night, under the command of One-Eyed John Monoco, a Nipmuc known by the colonists, over 400 warriors positioned themselves for an attack, with the majority of them hiding on the western slope of Gibbet Hill.

As the day dawned, the farmers moved out of the safety of the garrisons and began to attend to their overdue morning chores—milking the cows and setting out fodder. Two Indians presented themselves to the view of everyone and then turned and ran over Half Moon Meadow at the base of Gibbet Hill. The men in John Nutting's garrison emptied out after the Nipmuc. Seeing what was happening, some of the men of Captain Parker's garrison began to join in the chase. The men reached the base of Gibbet Hill and hundreds of armed warriors stood up and opened fired. In the rout that followed, one man was killed and three lay on the ground. Lucky for them, gun technology was horribly inaccurate then.

The volley had signaled to a second group of warriors on the opposite side of the garrisons, who pulled down the stockade fence and made their way toward the Parker garrison house. The farmers made it back to the Parker garrison safely and slammed the door before either group of warriors caught up to them. However, the triumphant Indians spent the whole day removing corn and plundering the household effects of five families from the Nutting garrison house, as the helpless owners watched.

One-Eyed John spent the night in the Nutting garrison house. He had the company of a few of his warriors but the majority spent the night in the meadow, dancing and singing around a fire. One-Eyed John shouted to Captain Parker and Captain Parker shouted back. John bemoaned the war with his old neighbor and suggested putting an end to it. He then boasted of his destruction of Lancaster five weeks before and vowed he'd burn all the towns between Groton and Boston. He taunted the farmers with the burning of their church. Their God had done nothing to stop him. In fact, the warriors had burned all the houses of Groton.

The next morning the 400 Nipmuc warriors marched out of town with impunity. They cut off the head of the slain man in the road and stuck it on a pole and turned his dead eyes toward the land he'd farmed. They dug up the corpse of the man killed the week before and cut off his head and leg and stuck it to a pole. An infant they'd found dead and abandoned in the first garrison, was cut up and fed to the pigs. Forty charred houses still smoked as the door to the Parker garrison was opened and the families emerged. The people of Groton packed up what belongings had been spared by the fires and retreated to Concord, Massachusetts, where many of them had relatives and friends. There they stayed until the spring of 1678, when they returned to Groton and began the business of rebuilding.

A legend remains of that day and night. During the main attack when the routed men were running toward the safety of the Parker garrison, it is said they passed right by the Nutting garrison house, forgetting that their wives and children were still inside. Seeing their men abandon them, the women flung open the door and ran screaming after them. They had never run so fast in all their lives, for right behind them was the entire Algonquin army. No one got any sleep that night.

The farmers fled with the aid of a company of horse soldiers under the command of Lieutenant Oaks. The followers of Monoco took advantage of their slow progress along the road to Concord and attacked them when they reached the Groton Ridges. Two more settlers died.

Many years later, travelers crossing over Gibbet Hill or the Groton Ridges at night tell of hearing the cries of the mothers and children (or is it the gibbeted pirate?). One such traveler, the well-known Revolutionary War soldier, Col. James Prescott, did hear eerie sounds as he was returning to town from Boston on a night under a full moon. Tying his horse, he hiked aways up the slope and found a pond beyond the Groton Ridges. He followed the screams to a litter of mink hungry for their absent mommy. I myself have often heard similar cries on many nights trying to sleep under an open window on Gibbet Hill. Those sounds turned out to be mating raccoons.

Oh, and bragging One-Eyed John was later captured by colonial soldiers and marched through Boston toward the gallows where he was gibbeted in September, 1676.

CHAPTER 3

THE BANCROFTS OF GROTON

EARLY NEW ENGLAND

The man who would one day build what is known as the castle on Gibbet Hill, General William Amos Bancroft, had descended from early New England settlers and he never failed to tell anyone who would listen.

Bancroft, as we shall see, did nothing on a small scale. His triumphs as well as his defeats were massive. Every time he ran for public office he won by a landslide. His famous Harvard crew didn't just beat Yale; they crossed the finish line with the trailing Yale scull nowhere in sight. Bancroft even died of a massive stroke. When the General began Shawfieldmont on Gibbet Hill, it was to be his family country estate, grander than the De Havilland French manor where his daughter lived, a monument to be passed down for generations.

The genealogy of his family is published in *The New England Historical and Genealogical Register*. The founder of the Bancrofts in the New World was named Thomas. He had come to Lynn from England, probably in the 1640s. Having lost his father and stepmother when he was 10, Thomas followed his brother to the colonies seeking a better life. He received a grant of land with the condition that he "improve" it within four years. It was a sentence of hard labor. With crude axes and saws these tough men erected spacious barns and very simple framed dwellings consisting of a huge fireplace with one large room attached.

Thomas Bancroft moved to Dedham, south of Boston, and was contracted to build part of the highway but got into trouble for failing to complete his task. In those days a man not completing a debt or contract could be thrown into "gaol" which could mean the doom of his family. Thomas made a deal with the town and worked off his commitment by hauling fencing to enclose the highway against wandering livestock. He was then free to move back to Reading in 1649.

His son, also named Thomas, was the first of the family to come to Groton in 1675 as a lieutenant in the Lynn Militia Company during

King Philip's War, He was one of 20 soldiers sent in November, 1675 to guard the garrisons at Groton and probably was there when the town was attacked and burned by Indians. Thomas went on to become a "man of substance." He served on the Essex Grand Jury and was constable of Lynn, both north of Boston.

Groton kept calling to the Bancrofts, however. Benjamin Bancroft moved from Charlestown to Groton around 1728 at the age of 27. He'd heard about the area from his father and grandfather, who had both been stationed there during the Indian Wars. By 1728 Groton had progressed away from its designation as a frontier town. The last of the French and Indian Wars had ended two years before, so the town was mostly safe from Indian attack*.

Benjamin brought with him a wife, two sons, and the marketable trade of tanning, a smelly but respectable profession, and a solid yeoman middling class. Benjamin bought a place just south of the present-day Unitarian Church on the east side of the Great Road (Route 119). The stone powder magazine used by the state during the Revolution was situated on his land. He soon served his new community as deacon of the church and town treasurer. He did so well he was able to eventually donate the land for one of the two independent schools in Groton—the Groton Academy, which eventually became Lawrence Academy.

He and his wife Anna Lawrence produced nine children of which only three survived into adulthood. Three of their little children died within a month in 1745, probably of measles, which killed scores of children in Boston before and after that year. Between 1732 and 1745 Anna buried six children in the Groton Old Burying Ground.

Taken to the Old Burying Ground

The Bancroft family has many headstones in the Groton Old

---

* Although in 1744 a lone warrior shot and killed a Groton farmer as he entered the gate to his yard.

Burying Ground, located between Hollis Street and School Street. The inscriptions were copied a hundred years ago by a student of Groton historian Dr. Samuel Green, and thank goodness, because much of the information on the Victorian marble has since melted away. Most of the markers are blue-gray slate, a perfect memorial for it is virtually indestructible. The inscribed block letters on these stones are as legible today as they were when they were carved, probably by someone with the last name Park. William Park and his sons carved eerie winged skulls, weeping willows, and giant urns on a majority of the historical headstones in Groton, Harvard, Pepperell and other towns in the area. Their own large stones are plain and undecorated. One of their descendants, Lawrence Park, would write the history of his family and—as we will see—design a house for William Amos Bancroft.

The gravestones record the names of families long resident in Groton. For example, a grouping of small headstones tucked in under messy pine trees tells a tragic tale. Beginning on September 2, 1753, four of the eight children belonging to Elisha and Elizabeth Rockwood began to die. Samuel, the first, was 12 years old. Pink, chubby Moses, only two months old, succumbed five days later. Two funerals in less than a week, yet the most horrible day of all was to come. Ten days later, Elizabeth, the oldest at age 15, and tiny Lydia, having turned six in May, passed away within hours of each other on September 17.

Elizabeth and Elisha Rockwood no doubt spent the night of September 17th begging their vengeful God to be merciful. Were they among God's elect? They must have blamed themselves and made appeal after appeal to God bargaining with a future of greater deprivation and penitence if only to save those remaining four children. Blessedly those four children did live and Elizabeth gave birth to five more, naming them Samuel, Elizabeth, Lydia, Sibell, and Sarah. Only the innocent infant Moses would not have a namesake.

The graveyard bears witness to the 1765 visit of a deadly childhood disease to the Groton's Prescott family. Six young cousins and one adult were struck in the fall of the year with throat distemper, known today as diphtheria. All U.S. children are vaccinated against it these days and no longer contract the disease. Diphtheria is caused by a bacterium that produces a nasty toxic protein. Bacterial toxins are seriously dangerous, and minute quantities in the blood are life-threatening. Even if properly treated, one out of every 10 people infected with diphtheria die. But in 16th century America it was particularly deadly. New Hampshire was incredibly hard hit. Over 1,000 died in 1735, 900 or so under 20 years of age. Twenty families in Hampton Falls lost ALL of their children. More than one-sixth of the inhabitants died within 13 months. In Haverhill, Mass, 256 children died between November 1735 and December 1737. Two hundred and ten of them were under 10 years old.

In 1765, Dr. Oliver Prescott lost two children and his brother, James, lost three. Their sister, Lucy, aged 37, also died. All of their slate gravestones bear the warning, "died of throat distemper." Perhaps Dr. Oliver had ventured into Boston and brought it home to his children who then shared it with their cousins. The youngest members of the family probably just keeled over before the family knew they were infected. After a few hours of suffering with a horribly painful and pussy throat, each one died. And died and died. A few other Groton families lost children from this outbreak but nothing like Haverhill and Hampton, for the local doctors had, by this time, learned how to stop this horror from spreading to the entire town. No one visited the Prescotts for months.

Country Doctor Amos Bancroft

Medical care in New England was improving by the time Benjamin Bancroft's second son, Edmund, bought a farm in the northwestern part of Groton, which became part of Pepperell in 1857. He produced 12 children from two wives, with only three dying in childhood. His ninth son Amos made his way into the world of learned men and became the first of the family to graduate from Harvard in 1791. Although this seems like an early year to have graduated from college in the United States, Harvard had been around since 1636. All the previous Bancrofts were working men. Amos's grandfather was a tanner; his great uncle, a shopkeeper; other relatives were innkeepers, boat captains, sailors, preachers, but most were farmers and soldiers, fighting in the Indian Wars, the Revolutionary War, the War of 1812, and the Civil War.

Amos founded the branch of the Bancroft family that would move into the upper ranks of society. Descendants would hold public office and academic degrees, and one would take over the Wall Street Journal. Amos received his Masters of Biology in 1794 and an M.D. from Harvard in 1811. He signed up to work with Dr. Isaac Hurd of Concord, MA, and then Dr. Oliver Prescott, the physician who had lost so many of his children to diphtheria.

In those days, country doctors took on students as apprentices before they graduated from medical school, which was more a general biology course than a true medical college as we understand it today. The college students were not allowed to work with cadavers and had no clinical experience. The real learning took place when they were interned with country doctors housed in the top floors of rambling farmhouses. Many of the students were teenagers and were looked after and given moral instruction by the hardworking doctor's wife.

Amos was the exception. He was 35 when he graduated from medical school. While living in Weston, his wife Abigail Whiting had died in 1799 at the age of 27, leaving a two-year-old daughter; maybe this loss had compelled Amos to study medicine with Dr. Prescott. He married again in 1800, to Sarah Bass of Boston, and had five children by the time he graduated from medical school. Since Amos's brother Thomas had inherited the farm in Pepperell after their eldest brother Edmund died of smallpox during the Revolutionary War, Amos brought his family home to stay in Groton after he established himself as a successful physician.

Dr. Bancroft became the best-known physician in the area. He would eventually take on many students himself, including George C. Shattuck, who will feature later in our story. During the deep New England winters, Dr. Bancroft would grab snowshoes from behind the door and head out to make his rounds. He was often away from home for days. Being a country doctor was no picnic but was better than working as a tanner.

Amos bought a pre-revolution home that had once belonged to his relative Timothy Bigelow* on the northside of Main Street with farmlands stretching into the Half Moon Meadows in the morning shadows of Gibbet Hill. His land included the large plot across the street which would eventually be the site of the Groton town hall. It stretched from Main Street to the train depot where the present day Groton Electric Light Company has its facility. The square block was known as the Lewis Lot. The house had a huge center chimney, common for its vintage, and a large barn in the back. By the 1870s a spindle fence fronted the street and an engaged column portico jutted out from the front door with a small "walk" above, updating the ancient house.

Amos had two daughters who married Harvard men, strengthening the blood tie to that institution. William, born in 1804, the second son, moved to New York City as an adult and Amos Bigelow Bancroft, the youngest, graduated from Harvard

---

*   Timothy Bigelow was related by marriage and lived in Groton from 1789 to 1807 after graduating from Harvard Law School. He practiced law there and went into politics; he was elected state representative and senator and was on the General Court. He was speaker of the Massachusetts House in 1805. He married Lucy Prescott, daughter of Dr. Oliver Prescott. Timothy's father, Col. Timothy Prescott was a Revolutionary War patriot. He also founded Montpelier, Vermont. The family came from Worcester. The Bancrofts, Bigelows, Prescotts, and Lawrences were all related by marriage and all played a part in the history of Gibbet Hill.

Medical School and worked in his father's practice soon after. He stayed at it for five years after his father had died.

Charles, the eldest son of Amos and the father of William Amos Bancroft, inherited the Bancroft farmland with the house in town when his father died, on July 12, 1848, from a freak accident. Charles would live there until his death in 1873. Now that he had a home of his own, 51-year-old Charles finally married. He chose a local girl, Lydia Emeline Spaulding of Dunstable, 20 years his junior, and he managed to produce three sons with the time he had left, one of whom died in infancy.

Nearing the end of his life in 1851, Charles sold a plot of land next to his on Main Street to George S. Boutwell, just elected governor of Massachusetts and a man destined to become a congressman in the Lincoln administration, secretary of the Treasury for President Grant, and finally a U. S. senator. The Boutwells had a farm adjacent to the Bancrofts' on Hollis Street. George Boutwell promptly built a house on the plot even though he occupied the governor's mansion in Boston. This house was owned by the Boutwell family until it was donated to the Groton Historical Society by daughter Georgianna to be run during the summer months as a charming old-fashioned town museum, with an upstairs room preserved exactly as it was when President Grant slept there in 1869. The scholar and historian Dr. Samuel Green lived in the house on the other side of the Boutwells'. In 1839 Charles' brother, Amos Bigelow Bancroft, built a posh Greek revival house across the street next to the town hall.

William Amos Bancroft

In 1855 Charles and Lydia's first son was born, and they named him William Amos, after his grandfather and uncles. When William was just two his infant brother Charles Herbert died. Two years later his brother and companion, Frederick Bigelow came along on June 7, 1859. The boys enjoyed growing up on a working farm of about 105 acres, 35 of which were adjacent to the house.

Young William was a vigorous lad, in contrast to his frail father. He and his brother Fred were boys during the glorious Civil War. Over 250 Groton men left for the south, among them Bancrofts, Spauldings, Shattucks, Parkers, Bloods, and Hazzards.* Along with all other children in town, Fred and Will must have watched the men from Company B, Sixth Regiment of Light Infantry of the MA Volunteer Militia march off down the Great Road toward Lowell. The Sixth Regiment traced a glorious lineage stretching back to the old Groton Artillery, first formed in 1775. William studied the great battles of the war and dreamed of one day joining the militia and following in the footsteps of the honorable men of his family. It was a proud day when 14-year-old William shook the hand of General U.S. Grant while he stood on Bancroft land.

The brothers had a wonderful childhood. They loved to sled down Gibbet Hill's steep slopes when Farmer Hall wasn't watching, or to ride out toward the Groton Ridges for a swim in Baddacock Pond on a hot summer's day. Every Sunday the family would walk the short block to the Orthodox Church and listen to the sermons of Rev. J. K. Aldrich. The large house on Main Street even had a skeleton in the shed. The boys knew that the bones had once hung on a stand in their grandfather's medical office but had no idea who the unlucky man had been. All they knew was that it was fun to scare the neighbor kids by opening the barrel where it was stored.

When it was time, William and his brother enrolled at the school for which their great-great-grandfather had given one-quarter acre of land in 1792. Founders Benjamin Bancroft and his brothers William and John, Dr. Oliver Prescott, Samuel Rockwood, John Park, Samuel Lawrence, Timothy Bigelow, Levi Kemp, and Isaiah

---

*   Adrastus Hazzard, enlisted at age 26 in Company F of the 54th Infantry Regiment Massachusetts, the first official Black unit in the United States armed forces. The 54th was depicted in the 1989 Academy-Award winning film *Glory* starring Matthew Broderick, Denzel Washington, and Morgan Freeman. Private Hazzard died with his unit on July 7, 1865, in Beaufort, South Carolina.

Hall had all contributed money to founding a seminary primarily for the preparation of Groton's educable boys.

In a petition to the Senate and House of Representatives of the Commonwealth of Massachusetts, these learned men and many others humbly observed, "the happiness of community requires the dissemination of knowledge and learning among all the classes of citizens. An enlightened people only can be expected to entertain a due regard for the great obligations of morality, to give that obedience to law necessary to good government, and permanently to adhere to those rights of men which are defined by a free and liberal constitution." The passed legislative bill came back from the state house signed by Governor John Hancock, one would assume in a large sprawling hand. By the time William became a student there, the Groton Academy had been renamed Lawrence Academy, thanks to significant donations from the Lawrence family. That was lucky as the other school in town was to be named Groton School. William would attend from 1867 to 1872.

On a winter day, possibly sometime in 1868, William Amos Bancroft looked up from his books in the library of Lawrence Academy and made a promise to himself. Gibbet Hill beckoned to him with its crops and cows and set him to daydreaming, making it hard to concentrate on Latin. Someday he would buy the hill and build a great mansion on its top, bigger than the Lawrence Estate on Farmer's Row and much grander than Governor Boutwell's house in town. He would join his father's farm with all the land up and over the hill all the way to the land holdings of his mother's family. From up there on the crest of the hill he would see the whole of Groton, the spires of the churches marking the snow-covered distance, first one and then back to the other, cold bells striking the hours clearly, the sinking sun streaking the sky orange. William's five years at Groton Academy gave him ample time to plan his estate.

In the fall of 1872, William loaded his belongings onto the train and made the 60-mile journey to begin advanced studies at the famous Phillips Exeter Academy in Exeter, New Hampshire. He returned to Groton in 1873 to attend the funeral of his father, after which the family home and most of the land was sold off to the Boutwells and others in 1875 since there was now no one left to farm the place. His kid brother, Frederick, had gone off to New York City.

William's mother moved to the Newton farm in Groton, 17 acres in total with a small house. With the change in his family's fortunes, Will supported himself by taking on odd jobs and farm work. He made a name for himself on the athletic fields, especially the gridiron where he "could send the ball further with his fist than the other players could kick it." William graduated Phillips Exeter in 1874 and enrolled at Harvard.

The Rise of W. A. Bancroft

William brought his mother to live with him in Cambridge. They boarded with a widow, Martha A. Thayer, on 12 Ellery Street in Brattle Square, very near his classrooms. Due to his diminished circumstances he went to work reporting for the Boston newspapers, an acceptable job in light of his background. He rowed for the Harvard crew and would earn himself a spot in the Harvard Varsity Club Hall of Fame.

Bancroft's fame with rowing and his leadership abilities brought him social popularity, and he joined a network of clubs and organizations at the university. He was a member of the Hasty Pudding Club (the guys who dress in drag once a year and invite famous actors), the A.D. Club, the Institute of 1770, and the Everett Athenæum where he served as an officer.

With his plate already extremely full, he fulfilled a lifelong ambition and followed in the footsteps of his idol Napoleon when he joined the military as a member of the Fifth Massachusetts Volunteer Militia. With his work ethic and attention to detail, Bancroft soon rose to the rank of captain in the Cambridge Company. His company was commended as the best in all the Massachusetts Militia.

Unfortunately, all of William's male role models would be dead before he proved his worth. His mythic grandfather Dr. Amos Bancroft had died before he was born, as did his grandmother Sarah. William had heard the tragic story of his death many times. While crossing State Street in Boston, this vigorous man had been cut down with a blow to the head by the shaft of a wagon, a few blocks from where William would one day have his law offices. Ironically, Dr. Bancroft was attended to in his last few hours by his student and friend, Dr. George C. Shattuck.

William's father, Charles, died at age 71, when William was 18 years old and his beloved uncle Amos Bigelow would die on holiday in Florence, Italy, in 1879, a little over a year after William's first son, Hugh, was born. Only his mother, Lydia Spaulding, would live to see him rise to the rank of colonel of the Militia. After the Spanish–American War, where Bancroft saw absolutely no action because he hated the way things were organized in Florida, he was appointed major-general by Governor Crane.

In 1878, Bancroft graduated with a Bachelor of Arts and enrolled at the Harvard Law School. He became a proctor, reported for the newspapers, and coached his beloved crew. He also got married during his first winter in law school. *The Harvard Graduates' Magazine* writes, "In this, as in everything else, he kept his own counsel; and those at the same club table had no idea he contemplated this serious step until he failed to appear at the table and they read in the papers that he had been married." With a wife to support, he left law school and worked full-time. Keeping up his studies on his own he was able to pass the Suffolk Bar in 1881.

By the time he had passed the Bar, his wife Mary had two sons under the age of three, William immediately opened a law office in Boston with his friend and Harvard classmate Edward F. Johnson, who would become a judge of the District Court and mayor of Woburn. He continued to practice law until he was offered a position as superintendent of the Cambridge Street Railway in 1885. He rose to be general roadmaster of the West End Street Railway Company. While superintendent of the Cambridge street cars, he put down a workers' strike. *The Harvard Graduates' Magazine* writes:

> *This was a test in 1887 when, without warning, six hundred men employees of the road struck and walked out, leaving only six men, a woman, and a boy to take care of some sixteen hundred horses. By working day and night and employing every resource which he could command, he won the fight. The cars were stopped for only three days, the superintendent leading the first car that ran through the angry but admiring mob. Soon afterwards the West End Street Railway Company absorbed all the Boston car lines, and Bancroft was appointed roadmaster, and had charge of the construction of the first electric line of the company.*

Bancroft would work in the railroad business off and on for most of his adult life, but his real love was politics and he desired more than anything to be governor of Massachusetts. In 1890 therefore, he left the railroad business for six years to follow this political dream full-time. He was elected to the Cambridge Board of Aldermen that same year.

A powerful Republican, Bancroft managed to garner enough goodwill to get himself elected to the Common Council of Cambridge in 1882 when the city was run by a strong Democratic majority. He served as state representative from 1883 to 1885. In 1892, he was elected mayor of Cambridge by a landslide on a platform of temperance. Cambridge remained dry during his four years in office. He soon secured his reputation as a superb executive officer.

Always looking to higher office, Bancroft accepted the opportunity to preside over the 1893 Republican Convention and was a major speaker. Even with a great deal of political capital on his side, Bancroft was never able to close the deal with the Republican Party to become their candidate for governor, however, and he returned to the railroad business in 1896 as legal counsel for the Boston Elevated Railway Company. He was elected director and vice-president the following year. He had finally given in to pressure from his wife to leave politics forever. Bancroft would never run for elected office again.

ABOVE LEFT: Mary Shaw Bancroft, circa 1885.

ABOVE RIGHT: "Foxey" Bancroft in the crew uniform of Harvard University, circa 1876 (Harvard University Archives).

BELOW: William Amos Bancroft as Mayor of Cambridge, circa 1892.

Photo by P.H. Prescott. Gen. W. A. Bancroft, Bungalow, Groton, Mass.

CHAPTER 4

SHAWFIELDMONT

GENERAL BANCROFT BUILDS HIS DREAM HOUSE

Optimism was in the air when William Amos Bancroft began his grand estate, Shawfieldmont. Theodore Roosevelt's son Teddy Junior was a student at Groton School. Mrs. Edith Roosevelt was often in town to visit her son and take tea at the Groton Inn, the oldest in America. The Inn was known for an elegant silver-laden dining atmosphere and a lovely view of the most commanding spot in Groton, Gibbet Hill. The president of the United States watched the progress of Bancroft's estate on the hill with interest and undoubtedly made a few suggestions about colors, design, and, of course, size. Both had been overseers at Harvard for six years until Vice-President Theodore Roosevelt was promoted.

Bancroft had spent his childhood in Groton, and after his father's death in 1873, spent the next two decades amassing a fortune in Boston and Cambridge. When his mother died in 1895, he also inherited her small Groton farm. Bancroft and his family had enjoyed regular visits to the farm in the summers, taking advantage of the cooler temperatures and peaceful atmosphere. Now with money and power at his disposal, William Amos Bancroft, known as the General, was on a mission. He began to buy back his family's ancestral land and much of the connecting acreage. He started in 1897 by purchasing a house and barn and 15 acres that had once belonged to his maternal grandfather, Josiah Spaulding. Uncle Andrew Spaulding had inherited it from his sister, Lydia Bancroft, but had sold it two years ago to a family called Moyle.

In 1900, the General bought the farmland of his paternal grandfather, Amos Bancroft, the 35 acres his dad had inherited and plowed. He bought the rest of the Moyles' land (14 acres) and all of the Boutwell land (46 acres) and the buildings and land of Gibbet Hill from a descendant of farmer Joseph Hall (85 acres). He then bought all the land in between; a meadow each from Shumway, Richardson, and Gerrish (five, seven and 10 acres). He bought 25 acres from the Needham family. He completed the estate with the Benedict pasture on the top of Gibbet Hill (65 acres). When he was finished spending in 1902, the Bancroft patchwork quilt totaled over 325 acres. On September 13, 1902 the General purchased a burial plot high on a hill overlooking the new Groton cemetery adjoining Chicopee Row, indicating his eternal preference for the village of his birth. He then hired an architect and several contractors and finally began to build his dream estate.

He started in November with a fieldstone memorial gate on Main Street at the site of the General's boyhood home, which was completed by the end of May 1903. The *Groton Landmark* said the gate was "somewhat unusual for this area, but seen in Boston... favorable comments, attractive addition." The General appointed F. F. Low, M.I.T. class of 1894 and the chief draftsman for the architectural division of the Boston Elevated Company, to design the structure. Bancroft was now president of the Boston Elevated (the El) and ended up using all kinds of resources and why not–it was not a public company. Charles H. Dodge* of Groton and Boston was to act as the general building contractor. The massive wall was built with fieldstones from Bancroft land and was capped with gray granite purchased from H.E. Fletcher and Company of Westford. A bronze plaque was embedded in the stones reading "To the Fond Memory of Charles Bancroft 1802–1873, Lydia Emeline Spaulding Bancroft 1822–1895." The whole memorial is still there except for the massive swinging wooden gates attached to the fieldstone columns. These must have been impractical to maintain.

The townspeople received regular updates on the progress of the General's estate, a paragraph or two appearing regularly in the *Groton Landmark* with the header "SHAWFIELDMONT." On a par with the Roosevelts, every time the General was in town or his name appeared in the Boston papers, a mention was included in the *Groton Landmark*. Locals read with interest as the General was

---

* Charles H. Dodge was a master builder who built the Baddacook pumping station in 1897, the Groton Public Library in 1892, and ran the Groton Inn from 1906 to 1921.

appointed chief marshal of his graduating class's 25th anniversary ceremonies at Harvard or presided over the 120th anniversary dinner of his high school alma mater of Phillips Exeter Academy. Bancroft was tall and handsome and respectable. And a generous man. In October 1902 during a massive coal shortage Bancroft offered 10,000 tons of Boston El coal for sale at cost, far below the market price. He would use this goodwill gesture as a confirmation of his excellent character for the next 10 years.

General Bancroft landed yet another honor as Grand Marshall of the Veteran's Column in a parade lionizing Major General Joseph Hooker, hero of the Civil War, on June 25, 1903. The parade culminated at the Massachusetts State House grounds for the dedication of an equestrian statue of General Hooker by Daniel Chester French* and Edward C. Potter. A curious choice for honor, Joseph Hooker had been Lincoln's third attempt at commander for the Army of the Potomac but resigned after his first major battle, so badly was he beaten. However, he had secured his place in people's hearts with brave performances at Antietam and Fredericksburg and later under Grant and Sherman and Massachusetts was still proud of him. Escorted by the Massachusetts Volunteer Militia, the Veteran's Column was commanded by General Bancroft, the former temperance mayor of Cambridge, in whose care Cambridge went dry. The 8,000 to 9,000 soldiers marching in the Veteran's Column of the Hooker Parade included men from all the wars since the Civil including the Mexican War. With compassion, the Army agreed that this was to be the last parade in which veterans of the Civil War would be present, making them continue might kill them. The governor of Massachusetts, John L. Bates, rode at the head of the parade on a black horse. The streets were jammed with well-wishers as state

---

* Daniel Chester French was sculptor of the sitting Lincoln in the Lincoln Memorial, John Harvard at Harvard University, and the Minuteman Statue in Lexington as well as many others.

and city departments and many businesses gave employees the day off. Red, white and blue bunting hung from every lamppost.

The Gatehouse and the Grounds

In the spring of 1904, the General began construction of The Lodge, a fieldstone gatehouse set slightly back from Main Street just inside the memorial gates, which would later become a carriage house as the Shawfield estate was developed further. The *Groton Landmark* reported that it would be "quite expensive and will have some eight or ten rooms." Stones for the project had already been hauled to the plot from the rest of the property. Charles H. Dodge was again hired to do the work. The General's son Hugh visited in April to view its progress with his friend, Dr. Ken L. March, a chemistry instructor at Simmons College.

By July the top of The Lodge rose above the shrubbery. Work began on a funerary monument in Groton Cemetery, his eternal view from the top. Meanwhile, newly promoted Colonel Hugh and his sister Miss Catherine sailed off to "the other side" for a few weeks in an effort to cheer up Hugh, whose young wife Mary had passed away unexpectedly, and Hugh's brother Guy had just returned from Paris on the newly built Republic.

The Castle Completed

During the 1904–05 winter months, granite from the Fletcher quarry in Westford was shipped into town on the train and unloaded into sleighs drawn by four-horse teams and hauled up Gibbet Hill to the site of the next project, the bungalow. Large Chelmsford gray lintels for the windows were extremely heavy and moving them up the hill on snow was a much easier proposition than trying to get them up the hill in the mud season that would follow. The finished bungalow's eight-sided tower was to be topped by massive granite brackets, two to a side. At each corner were double thickness granite brackets which weighed several thousand pounds. Local farmers were hired and supplied the muscle and draft horse and oxen teams to get the job done.

Work on the Bancroft farmlands continued after the snow had gone. The fields were improved and the road up to the hill from Main Street was begun. The General returned to Groton the first Saturday in February 1905 to attend the funeral of his maternal aunt, Mrs. Andrew Spaulding, and visited a few times in the spring but he was occupied most of the summer with a wedding and a business trip to Europe. In the fall of 1906, the hill was drastically altered from its former appearance. Between 800 and 900 trees and shrubs were set out, of which 425 were fruit trees. The General used his connections in the railroads to haul 50 carloads of horse manure in tipcarts from the clogged streets of Cambridge. From the railhead in Ayer, this fertilizer was loaded into wagons then hauled to Groton and spread by hand on 40 acres of plowed fields. To this day, local farmers claim the fields of Gibbet Hill farms are unusually fertile.

The most ambitious earthwork on the General's property was the building of a road from the memorial gates on Main Street up to the top of Gibbet Hill. Local farmer Charles Raddin, who would one day buy back his handy work, supervised this Herculean task. The road was to take advantage of a land feature bisecting Half Moon Meadow called Captain Parker's Island, named for a friend of One-Eyed John Monoco. Captain Parker had grazed his animals on the Island and the two Indians who drew the colonial homesteaders into an ambush had first appeared on the spit of land.

James Brook is formed partly by the runoff of the Half Moon Meadow which skirts around the base of Gibbet Hill. To ensure that a road would not be washed out in spring, Mr. Raddin was therefore hired to engineer a series of cobblestone ditches and raised road beds connecting the gatehouse with Parker Island and again over Half Moon Meadow at the base of Gibbet Hill. Around 2,000 railroad ties were dumped at the freight depot in Ayer and hauled by man and horse to Groton to mark the edges of the road.

A "picturesque" cobblestone bridge was constructed across James Brook. Fast-growing Lombardy poplars and lilacs were planted to line the driveway. Later, in the mid-20th century, most of Captain Parker Island became Mayfield Drive, named for the family of the husband of Groton historian Virginia May.

The estate continued its transformation while its owners were away traveling. Bancroft farm manager Henry Fitzgerald plowed part of the hill and planted about 30 acres of Indian corn. Much of the rest was left as hay. The grass of Groton thrived on the Cambridge horse manure. The hay crop in 1910 was 350 tons! The road to the summit was completed by the end of the summer of 1906, allowing the next phase of the grand plan for Shawfieldmont to be started: laying of a foundation for the stone bungalow on the northwest crest of Gibbet Hill. Additional labor had been hired for the construction and skilled Italian stonemasons and construction workers were staying in the Fitzgerald house. The water main of the Groton Water Company was tapped in early September to furnish water to the farm, principally for mixing cement for the foundation before cold weather set in and work had to stop for the winter.

President and Mrs. Roosevelt visited Groton in mid-February of 1907. The commander-in-chief was enjoying enormous popularity and his visit was a real treat to the people of Groton. A year ago the eyes of the world had been focused on the wedding of his eldest daughter Alice to Congressman Nicholas Longworth. And just two months ago, Roosevelt had been awarded the Nobel Peace Prize for his efforts in settling the war between Russia and Japan. Taking formal tea at Groton Inn, the Roosevelts observed the progress of the Bancrofts' estate. By early April, the imported Italian laborers were busily banging away on projects all over Gibbet Hill.

Hawthorn hedges were set out along Lowell Road and up and over the hill toward the reservoir. Workmen raised massive fieldstone boulders into the walls of the bungalow and finally into the turreted tower. Huge timbers were erected on top of the walls into slots allowing for an expansive open room at the center of the bungalow with a 12-foot-high fieldstone fireplace as its focal point. After many months the stone bungalow was finally complete. The General and his family could now spend the summers in comfort as he oversaw the construction of the grand mansion "Shawfieldmont" he had planned further up the crest of the hill.

Bancroft's Bungalow

The structure now standing atop the south side of Gibbet Hill is known today as the "castle." Before the wooden parts of the building burned away in 1930, the castle tower was nestled within the roof of a structure that was a cross between an American Craftsman and Tudor bungalow. Even on postcards of the era, it is very difficult to get a feel for just how big this building really was.

A perfectly proportioned copy of its smaller craftsman cousin, the building on Gibbet Hill is a "bungalow" the same way the mansions of Newport, Rhode Island, are "cottages." A tall man could stand up on its windowsills, place his arms over his head, and still not touch the window header. When viewed from Main Street, the optical illusion remained intact by virtue of a complete lack of plant life around the foundation, which would have given away its actual dimensions.

The 1906 Bancroft house was a replica of THE hot new style of affordable American houses, which were not yet found anywhere in Groton. Craftsman houses fulfilled middle-class America's desire for a fashionable home that had previously been available only from architects. The bungalow was a home with wit and sophistication that could be built for a reasonable price. The movement reflected the growth of the middle-class and marked the first time serious architecture was found outside the wealthy. This bungalow was the leader in a revolution changing the way average Americans lived. As *American Bungalow Style* says, "Bungalows allowed people of modest means to achieve something they had long sought: respectability. With its special features – style, convenience, simplicity, sound construction, and excellent plumbing – the bungalow filled more than a need for shelter. It provided fulfillment of the American Dream."

Whereas most bungalows adhered to the basic tenet of the Art and Crafts aesthetic and harmonized with the surrounding nature by coexisting discreetly with the trees and rocks, the gigantic Bancroft bungalow shouted its presence on top of a hill for all to admire. William Amos Bancroft celebrated progress and the Industrial Age and yet ironically the house he built in Groton followed the architectural principles of men such as William Morris, C.F.A. Voysey, and W.R. Lethaby, who said, "Art is the humanity put into workmanship, the rest is slavery. The difference between a man-made work and a commercially-made work is like the difference between a gem and paste."

An Arts and Crafts Movement believing art and architecture must be utilitarian was at odds with the Aesthetic Movement that claimed "L'art pour l'art." General Bancroft, made rich by the Industrial Revolution, could afford art for art's sake. Morris & Company had exhibited at The Foreign Fair, an international trade fair held at Mechanics Hall in Boston during the winter of 1883–84. What both movements abhorred was the demoralizing nature of the Industrial Revolution. Oscar Wilde writes in his *Art and the Handicraftsman*, "Do you think, for instance, that we object to machinery? I tell you we reverence it; we reverence it when it does its proper work, when it relieves man from ignoble and soulless labor, not when it seeks to do that which is valuable only when wrought by the hands and hearts of men. Let us have no machine-made ornament at all; it is all bad and worthless and ugly. And let us not mistake the means of civilization for the end of civilization; steam-engine, telephone and the like, are all wonderful, but remember that their value depends entirely on the noble uses we make of them, on the noble spirit in which we employ them, not on the things themselves."

General Bancroft, for all his traditionalism, came to embrace all the miracles of the new century and its advancements. While

Bancroft loved the openness of the bungalow rooms, the rustic outdoorsy appointments, and masculine motifs, he had no idea that his beloved mission furniture and mica lamps were just the initial vibrations of a political change that would take away his fortune and his health.

Mary and the Summers in Groton

On April 11, 1908, the entire Bancroft family was in attendance at the wedding of Guy Bancroft to his childhood sweetheart, Charlotte Nickerson, best friend of his sister Catherine. Miss Charlotte was "tall, fine looking and accomplished with a charming personality." Hugh almost missed the wedding having been suffering all winter with a serious case of typhoid fever and having been critically ill for weeks. Soon after, however, he and his second wife Jane were cheered by the birth of his second daughter Jessie, on May 4. Jessie was christened at the St. Stephens Episcopal Church in Cohasset, with water brought back from the River Jordan by C. W. Barron, from an old English font which had been used to baptize Abe Lincoln.

With the bungalow now completed, the Bancrofts with granddaughter Mary and several servants began spending each summer on the hill. These idyllic summers between 1908 and 1912 were to be some of the happiest of Mary's adventurous life. Until the Shawfieldmont mansion was completed, the family would stay in the bungalow, which would later be converted into a carriage and servants' house. The tower would become the living quarters for the grooms and coachmen and the Bancrofts' spacious sitting room with its high open ceiling was suitable for large carriages.

Mary had graduated from the constant scrutiny of a nurse and freely roamed the 300-plus acre farm visiting with farm manager Henry Fitzgerald and his wife, who lived in the white clapboard farmhouse on Lowell Road that had once been the home of Joseph Hall. Mary's favorite companions were the little Tolles girls living in the house across the street from the farmhouse. Willard Tolles, the girls' father, was a regular handyman on the Bancroft farm. Their house was later occupied by the Mountain family and was eventually bought by the Lawrence Academy to house members of its faculty.

Alice and Olive Tolles and Mary loved to poke around the pond catching turtles and butterflies. Hide and seek among the tall corn stocks gave way to forages for bouquets of blue gentians, goldenrod, and asters. Mrs. Bancroft had a flower garden planted outside her window each summer filled with mignonettes, verbenas, zinnias, marigolds, nasturtiums, and rows and rows of fragrant sweet peas. Mary loved the smell so much she tried one time to stuff them up her nose.

The arrival of the summer neighbors on the hill was a welcomed sight in Groton. The Tolles family benefited from extra employment around the farm and Willard Tolles helped build the monument in the Groton Cemetery. The Tolles children remember the Bancrofts with fondness. The stone wall along Lowell Road was a favorite place for them to play. The General asked them to kindly pick as many roses as their little arms would carry when he was away, so the buds would keep coming and the lovely open ones would not go to waste. He also made a special point of making a trip to Groton the week before Christmas to hand-deliver presents for all the neighborhood children. A Santa Claus with a German Kaiser drooping mustache.

Farm life was a real-world education in contrast to the private schools Mary would attend her entire life, and she reveled in its freedom. She writes of stealing away to the reservoir pasture to inspect a newly dropped calf sired by the farm's ornery white bull with one brown eye and one blue eye. She watched as Fitz captured the black heifer and her calf and led them to the safety of the barn. General Bancroft's right-hand man, Thomas Nolan, later that day in the farmyard explained how the calf had come to be in the belly of the black heifer, put there by the white bull. That evening at dinner,

Mrs. Bancroft was appalled as Mary recounted her adventures with the dropped calf exclaiming it was unsuitable dinner conversation for a young lady. As we will see, bovine breeding would occupy another lady's attention on Gibbet Hill later in the century.

The family was seen each afternoon in their fine open victoria carriage on the streets of Groton or stopping at the train depot to meet a friend or family member arriving from Boston. Mrs. Bancroft was always fashionably turned out with her ruffled parasol tilted to protect her complexion from the harsh sunlight. Little Mary might be dressed in a white batiste dress with eyelet embroidery over a pink slip and on her head a hat with a crown of pink silk. Thomas Nolan served as driver on these occasions and wore a traditional gray broadcloth coachman's outfit with a high gray hat.

Hugh decided to retire from the Massachusetts Volunteers that winter. He had reached the rank of his father, major general. Like his father, Hugh had enlisted in Company B of the 5th Regiment as a private. After attaining his law degree, he had been promoted to the position of adjutant general and served on the staff of Governor Curtis Guild, Jr as chief of the Judicial Advocate General Department. The adjutant generalship is a major administrative position in the army which evolved, after the Spanish–American War, into a central bureau coordinating non-supply functions such as records, staff, programs, and policies.

Under military law both of the retired Bancroft generals were eligible to perform any military duty to the same extent as if they were not retired. They might be required to serve on military boards and courts of inquiry. Most fun of all, they were entitled to wear the full glorious uniform of their rank.

Happiness Before the Storm

The year 1912 dawned with General Will motoring out to meet his cousin from California, Mrs. Rising, at the Groton Inn. Soon after, the seventh Bancroft grandchild, Frederick Haviland, was born. It was a snowy winter in Massachusetts and Mr. and Mrs. Lawrence Park attended a lovely sleigh-riding party that began at the Groton Inn hosted by Miss Sarah Bancroft, the daughter of Dr. Amos Bigelow. With so much snow, the children of Groton took to coasting Gibbet Hill with their sleds. A local boy by the name of George Folkins bent his double runner on one trip down and broke his leg in two places.

But an event on February 16 foreshadowed what would become an *annus horribilis* for the Bancrofts. While riding in his town car, the General was struck by an inbound subway car at Harvard and Prospect in Cambridge. The chauffeur, J.B. Schooner managed to avoid serious injury but passenger Northern Division Superintendent George R. Tripp was seriously hurt.

At the end of May, Mrs. Bancroft came to Groton as usual to open up the estate for the summer. It was to be eight-year-old Mary's last summer there. However, as we will see, their plans soon had to change. Even though it turned out to be one of the hottest summers on record, the family stayed in Cambridge, unable to take advantage of the cool breezes on Gibbet Hill. President Bancroft of the Boston Elevated Railway had his hands full at the office.

ABOVE: Workman huts atop Gibbet Hill in 1897. The Groton Water Company began to lay pipe on Main Street and hired Italian immigrants. The unmarried employees lived in these hovels while the married workers lived in caravans with their families on Baddacook Pond. The master stonemasons built the reservoir just beyond the crest of Gibbet Hill and it is likely that many of these workers also helped to build the Bancroft Bungalow (Courtesy of Earl Carter).

BELOW: The canal system (Photo by the author, 2009).

LEFT: Hugh Bancroft, portrait by Blank & Stoller, published in the *Boston Herald* in September, 1925 (Herald-Traveler Photo Morgue, Boston Public Library).

BELOW: Mary Bancroft, circa 1961 (Blackstone studios, New York).

ABOVE: Gibbet Hill Morning (Photo by Sally Reed, May 22, 2023).

BELOW: Arborcroft, the Bancroft home, #12 Ware Street, Cambridge, street side (Cambridge Historical Society).

ABOVE: The Lodge on Main Street (Photo by the author, 2009).

BELOW: Cohasset Horse Show, left to right: F. Harold Tolman, W.J. McDonald, H. Hollen Crowell, William J. Davidson, Hugh Bancroft, Arthur Lewis (Leslie Jones, 1931, Herald-Traveler Photo Morgue, Boston Public Library).

ABOVE: Mary Bancroft and Olive Tolles (*Upside Down in the Magnolia Tree*, illustration by Paul Galdone).

BELOW: Postcard of the Bancroft Bungalow.

CHAPTER 5

THE END OF
THE LINE

SKELETONS IN THE ATTIC

Go to Massachusetts Historical Society in Boston and ask the librarian for a pasteboard box marked "Shattuck Family Papers" dated 1913 and you will find correspondence between General Bancroft and Dr. Frederick C. Shattuck of Marlboro Street, Boston. By this time, the beloved farm at Gibbet Hill had been sold and the General had returned to work as president of the Boston Elevated Railway after a leave of absence of over six weeks, his first vacation in 25 years.

No doubt Frederick's letter was meant to cheer up a man whom everyone believed had been broken by the events of the previous year. His grandfather George C. Shattuck had been a student of Dr. Amos Bancroft, the General's grandfather, and Frederick wanted to share with William a legendary story of his grandfather's early career. Thanks to this letter, William learned the name of the skeleton he and his brother had played with as children.

Samuel Frost*, a convicted murderer, was to be hanged on a hill in Worcester. Dr. Warren, a professor at Harvard University, had decided it was time to further Amos Bancroft's anatomy studies even though using cadavers was illegal at the time. Amos was talked into being a witness to the hanging of Frost on Halloween, 1793, and remained in town to mark his grave. Amos went back in the dead of night and dug Mr. Frost up. Discovered at his grisly work, Amos fired his pistol in the air to scare off the witness. The decomposing criminal was wrapped in a canvas, thrown in a wagon, brought back to Cambridge and presented to Dr. Warren, where Mr. Frost was carefully dissected and eventually rendered to just bones. The dead Mr. Frost then began a long career as an articulated classroom skeleton.

General Bancroft goes on in his thank you note to F.C. Shattuck:

---

*   In 1783, Samuel Frost brutally stabbed his father with a handspike. He blamed his father for the death of his mother four years earlier. Frost was acquitted of the murder by reason of insanity. Ten years later, he murdered his employer, Elisha Allen, this time with a hoe. Frost claimed Allen had treated him like a slave.

Of the highly prized remains of Samuel Frost I think I became cognizant at an early age. They reposed in the loft of the carriage house of Charles Bancroft (my father) during my boyhood, and were regarded by the children with something akin to indifference. There are several stories in connection therewith, which are amusing. I believe one was to the effect that they were at one time decently buried (of course long after my grandfather's death), and then accidently dug up in some farming operation by someone unacquainted with their antecedents, resulting in a suspicion of foul play. I have been told also that the skeleton was once a stake in a game of cards. What finally became of the thing I don't know, but I have the impression that Dr. Samuel A. Green has some information about it.

Massachusetts governor George Boutwell in his *Reminiscences of Sixty Years in Public Affairs* tells a bit more of the tale. When Boutwell was a student living next door to the Bancrofts, he studied Latin with William's uncle, Dr. Amos Bigelow Bancroft. He had seen the skeleton stored in the office closet. One Sunday afternoon during a ride with Dr. Bancroft, the two men were stopped by a neighbor, Asa Tarbell, as they were passing his house. Governor Boutwell writes, "After a little conversation Tarbell said 'I shall be over soon for Frost's skeleton.'" Dr. Amos, amazed, looked over and through his glasses, and said at length, "Why, what you mean?" Said Tarbell, "Some years ago, your father and I were playing, and I proposed to put up my uncle Ben against Frost. Your father agreed to the game, and I won. I told him I had no use for Frost at that time, and he might keep him."

One wonders whether Uncle Ben Tarbell had been alive or dead at the time of the wager. Either way he must have been of interest to the doctor. Uncle Ben had been a drummer boy in the Revolution and never grew to be more than the size of an 11-year-old child.

Many years later, when George Boutwell bought the Bancroft house in 1873, his foreman found a skeleton in a barrel in the shed and promptly buried it on the property, probably fearing an inquiry. Not content to lie in peace, Mr Frost was later plowed up and briefly played the role of the victim instead of the perpetrator of a murder.

Most of the farm hands were let go. Mrs. Grover Cleveland and her son Richard stopping at the Groton Inn heard the gossip of the General's misfortune. A week before the farm sold, the General was in town telling anyone who would listen he had decided not to sell.

The Boston El Strike of 1912

The morning of July 29, 1912, General Bancroft was to make a statement before the convened Grand Jury of Suffolk County, which was investigating charges of perjury, coercion, and interference with the rights of the El's employees to unionize. Twenty-five years before, in 1887, the General had put down an El union strike in Cambridge. The public had been behind him then. When a group of workers on the Cambridge and the South Boston Horse Railway made demands, he had immediately called in 150 men to keep the public service going. As superintendent he was responsible for the safety of each rider. When Cambridge police could not control the hoodlums stalking the streets of his city throwing bricks at passing street cars, the mayor of Cambridge allowed Bancroft to ready his company of militia, the City Guard.

The strike in 1912 had not played out the same way. This time, Bancroft appeared to be on the losing side. He had refused to acknowledge the union, just as he had so many years before, but this strike went on for over a month and service ground to a halt. Many citizens were seriously injured in the unrest and a few lost their lives. All this in the hottest Boston summer on record. And the politicians stood by and waited.

On July 26, headed by Governor Foss and Mayor "Honey Fitz", the Boston El eventually agreed to terms that ended the strike. Six

Elevated division superintendents were later indicted on charges of perjury by the Grand Jury. Most of the striking employees, save a few whose convictions for various acts of violence were not overturned in the courts, were reinstated by the El at their former positions. General William Amos Bancroft was never the same.

Going, Going, Sold!

Mrs. Bancroft and granddaughter Mary went out to Shawfieldmont probably for the last time on June 29, 1912 so little Mary could say goodbye to her beloved farm, her childhood friends, and that mean white bull. By September both Shawfieldmont and Arborcroft were openly advertised for sale in the Cambridge papers.

By the end of September Bancroft's estate was sold to speculator E.E. Tarbell and Mr. Kemp and Mr. Bennett of Pepperell. Two weeks later a huge auction was held. Everything else went including 65 head of cattle, seven horses, shoats, hens, hay, potatoes, corn, farming implements, and wagons. A crowd of locals attended the auction, all hoping to come away with a bargain. C.H. Green of Fitchburg bought 250 tons of hay at $20/ton in the barn. One span of horses went to a Mr. Keyes of Westford, and another to a Mr. Page of Pepperell, a single horse to Lunenburg, and another sold to S.P. McKean of Chicopee Row. One lonely horse was not sold. All the cattle were sold to buyers from a number of towns. The highest price was for a Holstein at $85 to Mr. Page of Pepperell. The poultry, all Rhode Island Reds, were divided into lots. Everything sold well–so well, the profit from the auction exceeded the selling price of the farm.

Bancroft was not present when the farm and all its contents were sold. He and his wife Mary booked passage on the Oceanic and were away for six weeks. They were in France when the sale happened. Like a bandaid, maybe he had just wanted to be ripped from his beloved dream quickly.

As soon as the Bancrofts had embarked on their ocean voyage, the rumor mill spun into action. There was speculation about why the General had sold his estate and whether his days were numbered at the Boston Elevated. On October 16, *The Boston Globe* reported that James L. Richards, who was on the executive committee of the Boston Elevated, denied he would replace Bancroft. Meanwhile, Hugh Bancroft, the General's eldest son, made a public statement that his father had sold the place because it required too much care alongside his heavy business responsibilities, so some thought he might have been forced to sell by his children. The fact that the week before he left for Europe, the General told everyone in town he was not going to sell the farm only fed the guesswork. As we shall see later, the real explanation seems to have been something else entirely.

Within a few days of returning to the States, William Amos made a trip out to Groton, to sign the papers from the sale.

Henry Fitzgerald, the beloved farm foreman, was without a job. He hadn't expected this. He was forced to board with his sister-in-law Mrs. William McMahan on Station Avenue in January, storing his household goods with Mrs. Smith of Mill Street. By April he had a job as a road commissioner and, by May, he had rented a tenement on Court Street, the street where the Bancroft house had been moved by Governor Boutwell. By August he had bought a house on West Street. He eventually sold his team of horses and bought a truck and worked at the paper mill like everyone else in town.

The bungalow became an expensive rental. The summer after it sold, it was rented by Harry H. Blunt of Nashua, New Hampshire. He was the treasurer at Wonalancet Company, manufacturers of cotton carding machinery. It was also rented out for parties and social functions.

The General returned to Groton from time to time. Nolan drove him out for the Memorial Day Parade and in August he attended the funeral of his cousin Miss Mary A. Bancroft, the eldest daughter of his uncle Dr. Amos Bigelow Bancroft. The General's family now summered on the North Shore —or, rather, Mrs. Bancroft summered there. The General still had his duties as president of the Boston El. In 1914, it was reported he was the largest-salaried corporate official in New England with a yearly income of $37,390. In 1916, at the age of 61, the General retired as president and was chosen chairman of the board. He retired altogether from the company the next year and, like so many active men who stop working, he began a slow decline. In 1919, he did dress up in his uniform and review the troops at Camp Bancroft, Boxford. Mary dragged him off to Riverside, California, the few winters he had left. He suffered a series of strokes beginning in 1920 and on March 11, 1922, died an invalid at Arborcroft, their Cambridge home. Mary is incorrectly listed in the paper as widow "Mary Shore Bancroft." Or perhaps not a mistake as "Shore" is more anglo than "Shaw."

The next day the Boston papers had a lot of nice things to say about William Amos Bancroft. The *Boston Herald's* eulogy was particularly touching:

> *Gen. Bancroft attained success over an extraordinarily wide range of interests, but in each case his three outstanding qualities largely contributed. They were an innate executive ability, tireless energy and fearlessness, either of ideas or of men. He was a stern man, but universally respected; quick to rebuke failure but equally alert to reward success; he possessed an almost limitless capacity for detail, and his name was a synonym for rugged honesty and a square deal. His driving power was enormous and on the river, in camp, in the mayor's chair, and in his business, the men behind him worked as a unit under his leadership.*

Nothing whatsoever was said about the strike.

ABOVE: Boston Elevated Railway employees during the strike of 1912 (Library of Congress).

BELOW: Boston Elevated Railroad Car, postcard.

ABOVE LEFT: John F. Fitzgerald, Mayor of Boston (Theo. C. Marceau, N.Y., Library of Congress).

ABOVE RIGHT: Major General William A. Bancroft.

BELOW: Inspection trip of the new Boylston Street subway on October 3, 1914. Bancroft retired two years later. From left to right: James Smith, superintendent of transportation; Pat McGovern; John Bright, major stockholder; Alderman Woods of Boston; car crewmen Sam Smith and Bob Power; Bancroft; M.C. Bush, vice-president; and Harry Nawn, contractor.

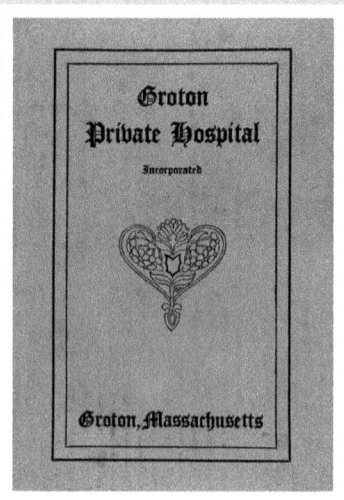

Groton
Private Hospital

Incorporated

Groton, Massachusetts

CHAPTER 6

DR. AYRES' HOSPITAL

THE GROTON PRIVATE HOSPITAL

Country doctor Harold W. Ayres bought the Bancroft bungalow on July 7, 1914, from a syndicate headed by William A. Kemp and Frank R. Bennett of Pepperell, who wisely held onto the mortgage. The first meeting of the Groton Private Hospital Incorporated took place that same day at four o'clock in the afternoon at 70 State Street, Boston. Franklin F. Phillips Jr., the other board member, was also present.

The incorporation papers described the primary nature of the business as a private hospital, sanatorium, and rest resort. Secondarily, the corporation could function as a public innkeeper. The good doctor had only been in town for a year, having left a practice in West Somerville. The Groton Private Hospital issued capital stock amounting to $30,000, with each share of preferred and common stock selling for $50. Later newspaper articles showed the medical facility opened for business soon afterwards. The first direct mention of the Groton Private Hospital in the local paper was July 1, 1916, a Mrs. Clapp had her appendix removed. That same year two barns were built north of the hospital building, where Dr. Ayres kept a stable of horses and a small herd of dairy cattle.

Over the next five years babies were born, sickness cured and injuries healed including those sustained while riding in the newest public health menace, the automobile. As Dr. Ayres' practice grew, The hospital produced an expensive eight-page brochure to attract business. The first page endorsed current medical thinking: clean air and hygienic conditions are as important for good health as the skills of the physician.

The private sanatorium movement was sweeping America and was a lucrative option for the country doctor. Most sanatoriums were a cross between a rehab center and a country club. Many of us are familiar with the classic movie version—the handsome consumptive hero playing backgammon on the lawn overlooking the Swiss Alps. While most of us associate sanatoriums with tuberculosis, the daily regimen of fresh air, exercise, and fresh chicken soup appealed to any chronically ill patient with enough money to afford it.

The Groton facility provided "every comfort for the welfare of the patient, there being a room devoted to lounging and reading and entertainment, measuring thirty-seven feet square, fitted with every convenience, private rooms, bath rooms, open plumbing, a charming dining room, billiard room, and a large sun-parlor 18 X 30..." All the ingredients for healthy meals were produced right there on the farm and meticulously analyzed water flowed down from the new Groton reservoir. The Guernsey cows supplying the milk had even won awards at the Groton Farmers and Mechanics Club Fair. "Golf links are provided and walks in every direction are charming beyond description." All this was priced at $20 ($200 in today's money) per week and included the nurse, treatment, and meals. Clean clothes and medicine were extra. What a bargain for anyone with a need for recuperation, other than the mentally ill and contagious. Consumption was not considered contagious in 1890.

Even so, hospitals were places to be avoided in the early 1900s. There was a widespread fear of formal medical facilities in every part of America. It is estimated that 90% of the sick in America were cared for at home after a visit from the local doctor carrying a black bag. Keeping beds full on hospital wards was a tricky business. Hospitals were forced to hire design firms and public relations professionals to convince the public that a sanatorium was a safe and luxurious place to recover. If necessary, private hospitals were willing to take in returning soldiers to make ends meet.

The War of the Lungs

The human species took a hit in the years 1918 and 1919. The Great War had exposed thousands of soldiers to poison gas and tuberculosis yet ironically, these were not the greatest threat to their health. As World War I was ending, a mysterious respiratory ailment began killing soldiers and civilians alike on an unprecedented scale.

Over 500,000 lost their lives in the United States alone—two and a half times as many as had died in combat. In the last week of October 1918, 2,700 Americans died on European battlefields compared with 21,000 civilians back home. Estimates state that 20 to 40 million people died worldwide.

The railroad from Boston to the powerful industrial center of Fitchburg, Massachusetts stopped at Ayer, making it an ideal staging area for troops waiting to go overseas. Camp Devens* in Ayer was established in 1917 and became the largest military installation in New England. The flu was ravaging Europe and hopped a ship heading for Boston in late August 1918. After landing at Commonwealth Pier it attacked naval barracks and training facilities. Within days it rode the train 40 miles out to Camp Devens and began its assault within the ranks of 50,000 helpless young soldiers, a good two weeks before it began to kill the civilians of Boston and Cambridge.

Camp Devens was the perfect killing field for the virus. Common victims were young vigorous men and women between the ages of 15 and 35. A soldier could be healthy one day and the next day be sick with a severe cold that rapidly progressed into a viscous pneumonia that began to drown its victims. Within hours patients' faces exhibited mahogany spots that extended to the rest of their bodies as the cyanosis developed. It was all over in a couple of days. The camp's doctors were swamped with dead bodies, 100 a day for weeks and they didn't have enough coffins or healthy personnel to deal with them. The trains took away the remains when a container could be requisitioned, but when it couldn't, the bodies were laid out in the barracks, in neat long rows.

With the train making daily trips between Groton and Ayer it was just a matter of days before the influenza spread into Groton

---

*   The area that included Camp Devens was a part of Groton until 1871 when it incorporated as the separate village of Ayer.

Center. Local papers began to report on the unusually high number of sick by mid-September, calling it the prevailing grippe. By mid-October, it had been dubbed the Spanish influenza.

A Charles Wright of Groton died the last week of September and the names of the sick and recovering began to be listed one after another in the newspapers. Over 50 people were identified by name in the next month and a half and hundreds of others probably suffered without identity. William Knapp of Groton, just 26, died at Camp Devens. Young Oric Bates ran off to enlist and was shipped to Camp Zachary Taylor, and died a few days later. Funerals were not allowed in public buildings, so the mourners of Irving Richmond Hendrickson, aged 29, held his memorial service outside. The Red Cross, the Grange, and the Women's Club suspended meetings. The town hall, churches, and schools closed. Young doctor Harold Ayres came down with the flu and entire families named Tolles, Lewis, Judd, and Wooley had no one well enough to make the noon meals.

Only eight people in town died of the Spanish flu, according to the papers. There may have been other deaths that for whatever reason were not listed, but the number was still relatively low. This is no doubt due to the previous virulent flu to hit the area in 1889-90. That outbreak had a similar infection rate but had a much lower death rate. Scientists have speculated that people aged about 15 to 35 in 1918 were too young to have acquired the full immunity from the earlier flu, whereas children under age 15 had acquired some immunity from their mothers' milk. Many of the young people had left town to enlist in the army, continue their education, or find work elsewhere, but this was little consolation for the family of mother and wife Clara Robinson Woods, who passed at age 25.

The Great Killer

World War I veterans not killed outright by the flu returned home in large numbers with severe lung damage from two sources. Over 70,000 suffered with poisonous gas wounds—30% of the total war casualties—and another 50,000 exhibited full-blown symptoms of pulmonary tuberculosis.

Known as the "Great Killer" or the "White Plague," tuberculosis is an infection caused by *Mycobacterium tuberculosis humanis*, a member of a large family of mainly harmless bacteria with one other notorious relative, leprosy. One hundred years ago about 90% of adults in America had been exposed to the bacilli, with only a few coming down with the disease, thanks to their immune system. Even today, 15% of the population will test positive for TB.

When TB bacilli are inhaled into the body, white blood cells immediately recognize them as foreign and either gobble them up or encase them without killing them, rendering them harmless for the time being. This is fortunate indeed for the bacterium. It takes advantage of the white blood cell and happily multiplies in its new home. When it reaches a critical mass, it pops out and spreads into the bloodstream. The spleen, liver, lymph nodes, and bone marrow have no trouble destroying the escaping bacteria, but the lungs, kidneys, long bones, and brain are often overwhelmed.

The immune system now familiar with *Mycobacterium* passes its valuable information to all white blood cells and when they brush up against the Myco antigen they aggressively attack. TB throws in the towel at this point in 85-90% of the cases. If any bacteria do remain alive, they are walled off in tubercle pockets lying dormant until they can strike another day. For the remaining 10%, the disease advances to its full clinical form. The tubercles liquefy and spill into adjacent tissues and the affected organ appears to eat itself. If it is in the lungs, the tissues needed for breathing dissolve and the patient exhibits the classic symptoms of a wet hacking cough and pink sputum in the hanky.

Tuberculosis has been killing humans for a long time, with evidence of the infection showing up in Egyptian mummies. It ebbed and flowed with time but by the middle 1800s it had reached a peak, killing every seventh person. Science identified it as contagion in 1865 and as a bacterium in 1882. By the early 1900s a diagnosis of tuberculosis was a slow death sentence. Treatments of the day carried with them isolation and stigma.

Since not everyone got TB, doctors thought there might be a tubercular personality-type. Physicians concluded that TB patients universally showed signs of antisocial behavior and sexual promiscuity. Dr. Maurice Fishberg speculated that a loss of self-control followed toxemia. As a result, patients became "selfish, and egotistic, often exhibiting moral indiscretions such as disobeying the rule about sexual commingling." It was also observed that artistic types were particularly susceptible. It was accepted that cultural giants like Poe, Keats, Thoreau, and Emerson might not have achieved genius had they not been sick with TB. More likely they were just bored. Nearly all physicians prescribed a regimen of complete rest, fresh air, and healthy food for TB patients. The only cure for hundreds of years was hygienic living. All that clean living drove the complex personality to misbehave. After a year of hell in the trenches on the Western Front, the last thing a soldier wanted was hours of inactivity, propped up with pillows, gazing at the pretty view.

Veterans' Bureau

Although national health care for veterans was not unknown, the quality of care was somewhere between inadequate and negligent. During the Revolution, the Continental Congress had promised a pension to soldiers in hopes of filling the ranks but medical care was provided directly by the states and varied accordingly. By the War of 1812, the government provided a domiciliary facility for the disabled vet but provided very little in the way of vocational training. After the War Between the States "Old Soldiers' Homes" were established, officially the National Asylum for Disabled Volunteer Soldiers and Sailors. Lincoln signed the legislation into law just six weeks before his assassination, making good on his second inaugural address promising to "bind up the nation's wounds; to care for him who shall have borne the battle and for his widow, and his orphan..."

Soon after the United States entered World War I, Congress provided for veterans benefits including insurance and pensions. The realities of caring for returning soldiers soon became a tangle, however, with dozens of state and federal agencies involved in the mess. In 1919 Congress charged the War Risk Insurance Bureau with caring for disabled soldiers, a task it turned over to the Public Health Service, a Treasury agency. Five agencies handled different aspects of veterans' issues and the processing of claims slowed immensely as demands grew.

In 1921, President Harding appointed two committees to look into the problem of all disabled veterans. He issued Executive Order 3669 on April 29, 1922, giving the newly established Veterans' Bureau access to the facilities of the Public Health Service; the War, Navy and Interior Departments; and the National Home for Disabled Volunteer Soldiers. With only 35 properties available to treat TB patients, the War Risk Bureau was given the authority to take out contracts with private institutions. Dr. Ayres' Groton Private Hospital held one of those contracts.

Dr. Ayres' Hospital was poised to take up the slack for the War Risk Insurance Bureau. After five years of relative indifference, the townspeople of Groton rallied around a charity tag sale raising funds for a new x-ray machine. With hard-fought public acknowledgment and six years of successful operation, in June 1920 Dr. Ayres signed his contract with the U.S. government to house and rehabilitate 40 World War I veterans suffering, according to the local paper, the effects of poison gas. In reality, Groton Private Hospital received soldiers who were infected with tuberculosis.

The U.S. Contract Hospital

Within three weeks 30 soldiers arrived. Caught up in efforts to consolidate medical treatment, the War Risk Insurance Bureau soon ordered five soldiers at the Groton Private Hospital to be moved to the government soldiers' home and hospital in Tongus, Maine. Director Chomley Jones, head of the War Risk Insurance Bureau, wanted to segregate the tubercular cases in federal facilities. The parents of the boys immediately protested to State Adjutant Leo A. Spillane to exert pressure on Washington to allow them to stay near their homes.

Whether sentiment overruled the town's fear of contagious diseases or people were blissfully unaware of the true nature of the condition of the new patients, by the fall the townswomen had formed a Red Cross committee to entertain the soldiers. They provided services such as mending and car rides. Handsome young vets bearing no outward appearance of disfigurement were soon whisked off with attractive young ladies as escorts to destinations such as the Army and Navy Club and the Majestic Theater in Boston. Care packages containing chocolates and tobacco were delivered to their door. The government had come around and decided to educate the boys, and sent vocational teachers from Washington, one of whom was Miss Agnes Scannell.

The next year was a happy one for soldiers and local girls. Military whist parties and Christmas gifts of house shoes, socks, and boxes of candied fruit filled the lonely hours of recovery and several romances matured into marriage. An Ernest McKenzie tied the knot with Miss Kennedy on February 2, 1921, at the Groton Congregational Church. Apparently a man in a uniform proved hard to resist even if he was coughing a bit.

In May, a group of patients took the four o'clock train to Pepperell only to turn around and catch the train back to Ayer. They were on a clandestine mission to decorate a train compartment with today's equivalent of tin cans and shaving cream. They had intentionally missed the Groton wedding ceremony of Elwood Macklin and Miss McKay, both nurses at the hospital, to surprise them at the Ayer station. The dear boys also handed the couple an envelope stuffed with money.

The newlyweds then boarded the train, took their festive seats, and traveled on to their final honeymoon destination, Worcester.

In 1921, a larger ward was built. The new hospital building, a 190-foot long ell, was placed on the crest of the hill facing west, affording a magnificent view and cold prevailing winds in winter. A long sun porch was added. It also housed a modern kitchen and dining room. The exterior was cased in fieldstones, harmonizing nicely with the former Bancroft bungalow and ensuring it would last until it was pulled down by Marion Campbell, who bought Gibbet Hill Farm in 1947.

The hospital also embarked on a campaign to win public opinion. It organized events that could be enjoyed by soldiers and citizens alike. The Saint Patrick's Day parade along Main Street marched to the beat of a U.S. Contract Hospital fife and drum corps. The town enjoyed open-air summer band concerts on Wednesday or Thursday evenings up on Gibbet Hill bedecked with lights. Yummy ice cream cones were sold to benefit the soldiers. The 13th Infantry Band from Camp Devens was booked for September 14, 1921. When the temperature turned colder, benefit movies were shown at the town hall and whist parties resumed. But by July 1922, the courtships began to sour.

An editorial appeared in the July 27, 1922 *Boston Herald* notifying the public that over 80 tubercular patients were being housed at the hospital under less than ideal conditions. Instead of warning the public, the letter was an appeal to raise $5,000 to construct a recreation hut. It pointed out that due to the nature of their illness, the patients required relaxation for treatment and recovery.

The building would house a small auditorium (theater) and stage on the main floor, with a reading room and pool room. Nurses would be quartered upstairs. The basement was to be divided into classrooms for vocational training and a garage for instruction of automobile repair and building construction. The local American

Legion Auxiliary immediately pledged money. The theater was brought over intact from Camp Devens and placed over a foundation. The recreation hut was located between the ell-shaped ward and the bungalow. Dr. Ayres continued to treat local patients in his fieldstone office building, built in 1919, east of the hospital.

Behind the scenes, a different picture was emerging. Throughout 1922 reports of the soldier's entertainments lessened and on February 25, 1923, an article in the *Boston Sunday Herald* under the heading "Rap conditions in Groton hospital" spelled out the coming doom. *The Herald* published a letter from William H. Burns, of the Massachusetts Association of Disabled Veterans of the World War to Colonel Edwin Ijams, acting national director of the Veterans' Bureau. Many complaints had been "received pertaining to the deplorable conditions at the U.S. Hospital at Groton." An immediate investigation was called for. Among the charges were insufficient heat and air circulation, and unsanitary conditions. The letter goes on to tell a grisly tale of soldiers being so cold they fought each other to snatch a blanket from those "who have passed on." It also claimed that the hospital was attempting to operate on 50¢ per day per man when the government was paying the hospital $4 per man.

Within two weeks, the Veterans' Bureau gave the order to "abandon" the hospital by May 14, 1923, and most of the tubercular soldiers would be moved to a new state-of-the-art government facility in Rutland, Massachusetts constructed at an estimated cost of $200,000. Chairman Halligan of the Rehabilitation Committee of the American Legion praised the Bureau's swift action in closing the hospital.

How had it come to this? Eighty-plus soldiers must have been a strain on the hospital's capacity with men two or three to a room. Groton historian Isabel Beal recalls her mother seeing the soldiers sitting outside on the porch of the small frame house on Gibbet Hill Road built as a residence for Dr. Ayres' parents. The general feeling in town by 1922 was one of disapproval of the moral character of the residents. The military whist games were probably accompanied by heavy gambling and drinking. Fathers had begun to worry about their daughters' honor. It was in fact the Groton Board of Health that made the complaint to the American Legion that led to the decommissioning of the hospital. Dr. Ayres maintained to the end of his life that he had done nothing wrong in the running of the facility. Between June 1, 1920, and May 15, 1923, Dr. Ayres' Hospital had treated nearly 400 World War I soldiers.

Veterans' Bureau Scandal

The Groton Private Hospital was not an isolated case. Public opinion began to turn in early 1922 with investigative reports in the *New York Times* and other papers uncovering one of the largest scandals in Harding's administration. Colonel A.A. Sprague, chairman of the American Legion's National Rehabilitation Committee, began a battle in the press with President Harding's private physician Brigadier General Charles D. Sawyer. As chief coordinator of the Hospitalization Board, Sawyer's principal job was to deny any problem existed in the Veterans' Bureau, citing an overabundance of available beds in the system. Sprague shot back with an eyewitness account of three men who were hospitalized in one room, one of them a mental health case, another a general surgical case, and the third suffering from tuberculosis. The mental health patient escaped and was brought back after wandering around town in his pajamas. He was returned to his room and murdered the tuberculosis patient with a chair (probably for coughing too much) while the surgical patient helplessly watched.

With a general atmosphere of graft and profiteering in the Harding White House, caring for veterans came under stringent scrutiny. The Merchants' Association of New York published a report stating "the men are not adequately cared for and many contract hospitals are described as positive menaces with insufficient restraints on the men and with gambling and immorality flourishing nearby." They claimed that the virtually unregulated contract hospital system was bound to become corrupt. Contract hospitals were profit-making enterprises in whose interest it was to retain patients as long as possible, rather than restore them to health.

The head of the Veterans' Bureau, Col. Charles R. Forbes, one of Harding's cronies from his days as a senator in Ohio, was often together with the president playing poker or making junketing trips to distant cities with cases of liquor and plenty of women. Forbes resigned in 1922 but not before investigative reporters Stanley Frost of *The Outlook* and Leighton H. Blood, in Hearst's *International*, had turned the spotlight of blame on him. Forbes had personally received thousands of dollars in kickbacks on hospital building projects and procurements of supplies. Tremendous quantities of gold were ordered for the filling of military teeth and had promptly disappeared. Buddies of Forbes' were being paid huge salaries for jobs they never did.

Colonel Forbes and J.W. Thompson, head of a contracting firm, were indicted in March of 1924. Warren Gamaliel Harding by this time was clear of prosecution, having died of food poisoning in August 1923. Forbes and Thompson were charged with conspiracy to commit bribery and to defraud the U.S. government. After a trial of more than nine weeks, they were sentenced to two years in prison and fined $10,000.

Were there actual abuses at the Groton Private Hospital or had the local American Legion lost faith in any U.S. contract hospital after the firestorm of scandal in the papers? The truth has died with the participants. Many of the soldiers were of Irish or Italian extraction at a time when local sentiment was squarely with Brahmin values. The Saint Patrick's Day parade may have fueled suspicion that the Irish were uncivilized drunks who gambled and caroused. There most certainly was a clash of culture between the patients on Gibbet Hill and residents below with many families forbidding members to associate with the veterans.

In 1921, the U.S. representative from the Groton district, John Jacob Rogers, told the 66th session of Congress what he had seen in Groton. In August, there had been 30 to 50 tubercular patients at the hospital. Rogers found that only four or five of them were receiving compensation from the government, "All of them were either trying to get or had thrown up their hands in disgust." He found that soldiers were sent to the hospital by the Public Health Service in Boston and then the War Risk Bureau was rejecting their claims for a number of reasons, including lost paperwork or denial that any disability existed. It took over six months for the award of aid to come through. Rogers entered into the record the plights of David Frank, Earl D. Nash, John Joseph Fitten, Anthony Salvatore, Frederick C. Peters, Sam Sacco, John L. Duffy, Michael J. Manning, Harry J. Cyr, and Ralph J. Feeney who were uncompensated patients in the facility.

Representative Rogers introduced the Rogers Bill or H.R. 14961 to establish in the Interior Department a "bureau of veteran reestablishment and for other purposes." Thus, what he had seen in Groton Private Hospital led to the formation of the Veterans' Bureau, which still exists today.

As a result of losing the government contract, the Groton hospital went out of business. Albert M. Phelps bought the hospital mortgage from William A. Kemp and Frank R. Bennett on September 29, 1924, for $4,970.90 and then acquired the hospital buildings and land outright from Ayres at auction on September 30, 1927, for $10,000.

Dr. Ayres kept the gabled fieldstone house and barn built in 1919 on Gibbet Hill and continued to raise dairy cows. He still had an office on the first floor and delivered many of the town's babies over the next 20 years. Groton historian Helen McCarthy Sawyer described him as unhurried, with a tongue depressor sticking out of his pocket, pausing often in his day to chat about the daily gossip or offer advice. He was educated at Harvard yet he presented a rustic character in keeping with his lifelong vocation of country doctor. His parents lived out their lives in the frame house on Gibbet Hill Road. They both died in the same month in 1927, and soon after the house was sold at auction.

Dr. Harold Ayres went on to care for Groton citizens until the 1960s and was given an honorary dinner in 1961 attended by hundreds of Nashoba Valley residents. He even started the Groton Rotary Club. A tall man, over six feet, he was kindly and unpretentious. A local man whose first child was delivered by Dr. Ayres remembers his hands were always dirty. Dr. Ayres was a great resource to the community.

Dr. Ayres eventually rented out the gabled house, which contained two apartments, and moved to a three-story brick end house in the center of town on the corner of Longhill Road and Main Street with his wife Pauline Lakin. His farm manager Karl Anderson lived in one of the apartments in the gabled house but suddenly left in the fall of 1944, before it was discovered that he had been taking out all the copper heating pipes to sell as scrap for the war effort.

Groton Private Hospital
Incorporated

Groton, Massachusetts

DR. HAROLD W. AYRES, Superintendent

A CELEBRATED physician, carried a patient through a serious illness, using all the skill of his chosen profession. The patient upon recovery, bestowed great praise upon the practitioner, who in reply told him that the credit should be shared with nature, his silent partner. The

Groton Private Hospital Brochure, printed about 1915. Top is the first page and the bottom is the billiards room.

Top photo is the porch with view of mountains and bottom is the second floor sitting room in the Bungalow showing the fieldstone fireplace.

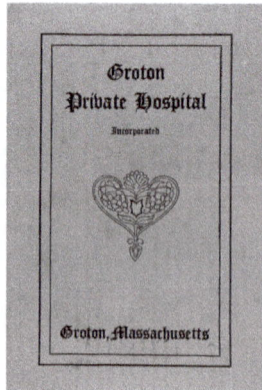

ABOVE LEFT: Cover of the Groton Private Hospital Brochure, printed about 1915.

ABOVE RIGHT: Postcard of the Groton Private Hospital c 1920.

BELOW: Hospital Complex in 1931. 1) Main Hospital Building 2) Recreation Hut 3) Dairy barns 4) Ayres' Home and Offices 5) Bungalow (in ruins) 6) Town Reservoir (Boston Evening Transcript, Boston Athenæum).

ABOVE: Top to Bottom: Bungalow Ruin, Recreation Hunt, Main Hospital Building (Courtesy of Earl Carter).

ABOVE: The gabled house on Gibbet Hill Road as seen from the bungalow ruin, once the office of Dr. Ayres (Photo by the author, 2007).

CHAPTER 7

BURNING CROSS

THE MEETING OF THE HOODED MEN

Heavy dark cars began to pull off the road within sight of Fitch's Bridge in northwest Groton, not far from the site of the Indian trading post of John Tinker. Bumping and rolling into a mown field of corn stocks left behind after the September harvest, the Fords and Dodges settled to a stop and the occupants quietly got out of their cars and pulled on their hoods. The sounds of doors shutting and low voices mingled with the crunching of boots over dried fodder. A short distance away, men in gleaming state police uniforms stood silently beside their patrol cars. They were there to protect the sheeted townsmen from outsiders. Lights from low beams pointed the way to a small fire where figures like children on Halloween night formed a circle and began to chant the creeds of membership. By the time the speeches started, 50 cars had surrounded the pasture. It was Wednesday October 13, 1924.

The men present had Yankee heritage and Protestant religion in common. They were ordinary Nashoba Valley citizens with occupations like dentist, mechanic, farmer, and shop owner. The very future of the old American race had fallen squarely on their shoulders and they were gathered together to uphold shared principals. The slogans they chanted encompassed a spirit of loyalty to the pioneer traditions of America: "Native, white and Protestant supremacy."

The Second Wave of the Klan

"America for Americans" political movements appear at surprisingly regular intervals all through U.S. history, vilifying progressive ideals, seeking in one form or another to insure that power remains in the hands of the crusaders of Christian values as determined by the "true" Americans. In the words of Hiram Wesley Evans, Imperial Wizard and Emperor, Knights of the Ku Klux Klan, these men must preserve and develop "America first and chiefly for the benefit of the children of the pioneers who made America."

This second incarnation of the KKK had little connection to the original group that had formed in Pulaski, Tennessee, after the

Civil War. The first southern secret society based its name on the Greek word for circle, *kyklos*, a nod to the aesthetics of plantation life. It began as a fun activity for a group of bored young men but soon morphed into a hidden police force chartered to oppose the influence of reconstruction politicians and to prevent the mingling of the races. Its membership drew from the best families and the Southern Democratic Party, their reign of terror only lasted six years.

Begun in 1915, the second wave of the Ku Klux Klan was an almost exact replica of the Know Nothing Party first organized in 1852. Like many men's organizations of the time, (e.g. Knights of Pythias, Odd Fellows, and the Masons), the Know Nothings insisted on fraternal order secrecy—the special handshake, password, and elaborate rituals endlessly fascinating to the good fathers of small towns. The party platform openly opposed naturalization of immigrants and the spread of Catholicism. When members were confronted with questions about the movement, each was instructed to reply, "I know nothing."

The Birth of a Nation

One reason for a resurgence of the original KKK of 1865 was a popular novel and play, *The Clansman*, first published in 1905 by Rev. Thomas Dixon, Jr. The unknown Hollywood director, D.W. Griffith brought the popular play to the big screen in California in January 1915. For its world debut in New York three months later, it was re-titled *Birth of a Nation*, in hopes of softening its controversial message.

Griffith created a film masterpiece still numbered today in most of the top 100 best American movies lists, making it uncomfortably unforgettable. Almost three hours in length, the epic contained dozens of cinematic achievements, including several tinted color sequences, which influenced every film project to follow. Charging the exorbitant price of $2 per ticket it showed to packed houses, smashing all box-office records. Even after the introduction of the talkies, this silent film made over $18 million and out-grossed any other film, sound or not, until Snow White and the Seven Dwarfs in 1937.

Even so, its technical brilliance conflicted mightily with its provoking message. The inflammatory portrayal of Blacks resulted in two scenes being cut, one a love scene between a reconstructionist senator and his dark-skinned mistress. However, this was not enough to prevent a virtual riot at the Tremont Theater in Boston. On April 17, 1915, 500 Negroes led by W. Monroe Trotter stormed the box office demanding tickets. Management refused, claiming all the seats had been booked in advance. The New York Times reported that Trotter and his friends, some of whom were white, "assumed such an attitude" that the manager was forced to call in the police. Six arrests were made and the lobby subsequently cleared so that the show could go on.

With riots also breaking out in Philadelphia, other major cities—including Chicago, Denver, Pittsburgh, and St. Louis—decided to avoid trouble by blocking the release of the movie. Nothing helps ticket sales like censorship and theater owners found ways around the ban. The landmark film emboldened white supremacy sympathizers who eagerly recruited founding members, culminating in the reincarnation of the dreaded White Knights.

The Ku Klux Klan

A sensational southern murder case fueled the fire. Leo Frank, a New York Jew, had been tried and sentenced to hang on October 10, 1913, for the murder of 13-year-old Mary Phagan in Atlanta, Georgia. Several years later Georgia governor John Slaton commuted Frank's sentence to life in prison, based on additional evidence. On August 15, 1915, 25 men attacked the Milledgeville, Georgia, state penitentiary. The mob seized Frank and took him to Marietta where he was lynched from a tree limb with his upper torso covered in white cloth.

Three months later, failed minister William Joseph Simmons invited a few active participants in the Frank lynching to a little meeting. "Colonel" Simmons had made a fortune recruiting for fraternal organizations. He had been a member of the Masons, the Knights of Pythias, the Odd Fellows, and the Woodmen of the World, so he was extremely knowledgeable about what ceremonies and trappings brought up the blood in other men. He had long held a dream of creating his own mystical order. He designed emblems and rituals while recovering from an automobile accident and went so far as to copyright his name in anticipation of future glory. After the widely publicized vigilante incident in Marietta, Simmons saw his opportunity.

Taking advantage of the celebrity status of the Knights of Mary Phagan in Georgia, Simmons reasoned their involvement in his new organization would take him to the next level. He had been previously recruiting followers among lodge members with mild results. Simmons devised a little theater for the prospective members atop Stone Mountain, Georgia on a chilly Thanksgiving night. The recruits built a small altar out of rocks where Simmons placed Old Glory, the Bible, and a sword. In the light of a burning 16-foot cross, the charter members dedicated themselves to "those principles of Americanism embodied in the Constitution of the United States." After being consecrated, the solemn group swore to uphold the tenet of the Christian Protestant religion and pledged to eternally maintain white supremacy. The next chapter of the Knights of the Ku Klux Klan was officially formed.

In 1982 terminally ill Alonzo Mann, a former office boy at the National Pencil Factory, came forward with the truth about the murder. Watchman Newt Lee had discovered the body of Mary Phagan in the factory basement. Mann had seen Jim Conley, a janitor and primary witness in the 1913 trial, carrying the body of Mary Phagan by himself. The state of Georgia had convicted an innocent Leo Frank.

The Klan grew slowly in the south made up mostly of the rowdy and nostalgic. The numbers began to swell when a few powerful orators learned the advantages of selling "hate at $10 a package." With an almost universal condemnation of these tactics and trouble with its administration, the KKK began a reform movement from within spearheaded by the intelligent Imperial Wizard Hiram Wesley Evans after first ousting "Colonel" Simmons. Miraculously, Evans salvaged the reputation of the Klan and began a campaign of such compelling rhetoric that he convinced hundreds of thousands to join his ranks.

Evans' arguments stayed away from inflammatory statements of open hostility and instead built upon the vanity of small powerless men. He explained to them that based on the "scientific" evidence of men like Lothrop Stoddard and Madison Grant, old stock Americans were inherently superior in breeding when compared to the "mongrelized Liberals." Aliens were unfit to rule and must not be allowed to do so. Bolshevist ideals of "produce as little as you can, beg or steal from those who do produce, and kill the producer for thinking he is better than you" were at the root of a failing America. With a falling birth rate and unchecked immigration, the low standards of the alien races were poised to overturn the long-held Puritan ideals of the founding fathers. The Nordic race as it existed in America had an obligation to preserve the integrity of the white civilization.

It worked. By the mid-1920s the Klan claimed a membership of over three million. In August of 1925, over 50,000 robed men and women peacefully marched on Washington. The conditions of their appearance included a lifting of the hoods to show their faces. H.L. Mencken writes in the New York Sun: "The Klan put it all over its enemies. The parade was grander and gaudier, by far than anything the wizards had prophesied. It was longer, it was thicker, it was higher in tone...The Imperial Wizard, Mr. Evans, was in it, but he profest to be only a guest. One tale has it that the Klansmen of the North organized the show to annoy and dismay their brethren in the South."

The Klan in New England

The reinvented Northern Klan was a Republican society opposed to the influence of the Catholic Pope, Jewish commerce, and the few Negroes in eastern cities. In the summer of 1921 only one chapter, or klavern, existed in New England. By 1922, groups had formed in New Haven and Hartford, Boston and Worcester, and several suburbs outside of New York City. Some historians believe growth was slow due to Yankee fears that the Klan would drive traditionally Republican French-Canadians and Italians into powerful Boston mayor Michael Curley's Democratic fold.

To the horror of American Civil Liberties Union members, Curley illegally barred any meeting of the Klan on his turf, even in private homes. The Boston papers hammered away at the Klansmen and bricks ended up through the Cambridge windows of suspected leaders of what became known as the Invisible Empire. A master showman, Mayor Curley ordered his policemen to set fire to crosses during his speeches so he could point to the icon and shout to the converted: "There it burns, the cross of hatred upon which Our Lord, Jesus Christ, was crucified..."

The anti-alienist movement in New England was not a social club for unschooled rednecks of the Yankee subclass. A highly intellectual discussion was centered on Harvard-educated Lothrop Stoddard and his 1922 book, *The Rising Tide of Color Against White World Supremacy.* The book warns that "unless precautionary measures are taken" the white race is in danger of being absorbed into a world filled with darker-skinned people. This deep-seated fear of dilution could only be allayed by the purification of America, a Freudian concept dear to the unconscious Puritan mind.

The Boston House of Representatives passed a resolution in 1923 proclaiming the Klan was dangerous to American civil rights.

At the Democratic state convention, the Klan was rejected by name. The Republicans, however, managed to avoid mentioning the Klan at all in their platform. Far from the immigrant-saturated capital of Massachusetts, Worcester was the logical center for Klan activity. Its spread was assured in the small towns of central and western Massachusetts, where the population was nearly 90% Protestant and old stock.

The 1924 Democratic Convention in New York became known as the "klanbake" by the national press with its replay of the Civil War. The new Union Army of the north offered up Al Smith, governor of New York and a Catholic opponent of Prohibition. The south and west backed former Treasury secretary William Gibbs McAdoo, a Protestant who was chummy with the KKK. Within three days the voting was deadlocked. In response, 20,000 Klan supporters drove off to a fourth of July picnic where they dressed in white hoods and threw baseballs at a stuffed Al Smith doll. After a rousing patriotic speech denouncing the "clownvention in Jew York," the tasteless delegates finished the evening with a cross burning. The Democratic party eventually nominated a candidate no one remembers (John Davis), who lost to the Republican incumbent Calvin Coolidge after the disgusted Democratic rank and file mostly stayed home.

The fighting at the convention was reflected in towns all over Massachusetts. Violence was reported primarily in Worcester County but also took place in Middlesex, Norfolk, and Essex counties. The same scenario was repeated in each village. Cars would gather after dusk in a farmer's field outside of town and hooded Klansmen would emerge forming a circle where low chants and secret ceremonial steps would intrigue locals milling about at the edges, many creeping in for a closer look. Several hundred satin-robed knights would burn a cross to signal the end of their meetings. This was usually too much for the small-town boys straining in the shadows. Someone would shout a nasty remark and throw a rock and an energetic melee would commence.

Riots broke out in Spencer and Lancaster. On a hot July night in Lancaster, not too far from Groton, 200 mostly respectable Klansmen feared for their lives for nine hours behind a police barricade as an irritable crowd tried to rip them to shreds. A brawl in Groveland sent three men to the hospital, where buckshot was extracted from their behinds. The jails in central Massachusetts swelled. As ten thousand Klansmen gathered in Worcester for a regional meeting, an airplane carrying delegates was shot down with a rifle. Invisible Empire automobiles were stoned and members assaulted.

Klansmen were also guilty of dishing out the violence. After a particularly inspiring meeting, members of the Klan who had been stoned three weeks earlier in Northbridge beat up two locals and turned over cars.

The Klan and Gibbet Hill

Clashes between the "Americans" and the "foreign mob" reached their peak in 1925. Rev. Arthur V. Dimock asked why some Protestants were "antagonistic to the society known as the KKK" at a meeting of the Groton Congregational Church. Surprisingly little else was mentioned in the Groton newspapers except for an editorial by Thomas H. Connolly on March 25, 1925. He described an incident where the fire department had to be called. Connolly found small scraps of oil-soaked burlap after investigating a claim that a cross had been burning on Gibbet Hill. He blasted the perpetrators.

These so-called men of the snake-in-the-grass variety, whose actions are so contemptible they hide their own faces, seek to destroy the principals which our great Americans like Washington, Lincoln, Henry and all the others laid down their lives for...there are no real Americans associated with these burners of the cross. No, the real Americans are above that and detest the tactics these people employ.

On an early spring night several young people were gathered at the parish house of the First Parish Church in Groton for a meeting of the Young People's Religious Union. The back windows of the hundred-year-old clapboard house had a perfect view of Gibbet Hill to the northeast. A member of the group, Olive Tolles, recalled seeing 20 to 30 men in white robes and hoods on the hill erecting a 20-foot cross and setting it on fire. The teenagers huddled in fear, unsure of the identity of the men under the robes. No one really knew who the Klansmen were in town, so everyone was suspicious. Ollie remembers that it was a scary summer in Groton. She and her friends couldn't help but think, "What was the world coming to?"

The logical target for the Groton Klansmen was the growing Catholic population. Very few Blacks lived in town and those who did claimed roots going back to revolutionary times. The Sacred Heart Church took its place along Groton's Main Street with the Baptists, Congregationalists, and Unitarians. The lovely stucco church had been a gift of William Amory Gardner. It had been the chapel for Groton School until Gardner's plans for a memorial to his brother who had committed suicide could be completed. When construction on the permanent chapel began, the old structure had to be moved. It was rolled on logs down Old Ayer Road pulled by a team of horses and set into place on September 27, 1904. The Episcopalians continued to be supportive of its mother church, albeit in private, as public opinion weighed-in on the KKK issue. Rev. Endicott Peabody wrote to a friend in 1919 that to his "mind the existence of a secret lawless society for the purpose of establishing democratic ideas is simply preposterous."

Groton made the New York Times on July 8, 1926, when Groton Parish Priest Father Mitchell sent a petition to the State Public Utility Commission to provide the church with electricity. Groton Electric Light Commission had cut the lights to the church the past Sunday because the church had refused to allow one of the meter readers to come into the church because he was a known Klansman. The

Sacred Heart's attorney, Joseph P. Walsh, suggested that the church install a meter on the outside of the chapel and the Groton Commission finally agreed to let the work be done by an employee of neighboring Pepperell's Lighting Plant.

While the Klan had fizzled in most of New England, Groton was considered a stronghold of what was left. The Klan made a bid to take over the running of the Groton government in 1927. A slate of candidates for town offices emerged that either were openly Klan or welcomed the support of the organization. Klanidates ran for selectman, treasurer, tree warden, electric light commission, town constable, and school board. They were members of some of the most respected families of Groton: Lawrence, Blood, Fletcher, Boynton, Gerrish, and Buckingham. If they were successful Groton would be held up as the "real Klan pioneer town of the Commonwealth."

In the February 12 election the Klan was partially successful. They won the races for treasurer, electric light commissioner, and two of three constables. A letter by Frederick G. May in the previous week's paper may have helped to sway Groton citizens to vote with their hearts and not their fears. May had disavowed membership in the secret society and "urged voters to consider town welfare" and vote for the most suitable candidates.

Perhaps the saddest consequence of Groton's flirtation with white supremacy was the demise of the venerable Farmers and Mechanics Club Fair. It had been a community institution beloved by all since 1860, but a take over of the Fair's governance by the Klan preceded the forcing out of John Donlon, the son of immigrant Patrick Donlon Jr., who had bequeathed his spot on the board of directors to John. As a result, angered locals boycotted the fair and farmers withheld their exhibits. The Groton fair ceased to exist, never to be revived.

The zealous nature of the old Yankee families had served the fair well during the plantation days, the Revolution, and the

War Between the States, but as in most organisms, something that becomes inflexible will most likely lead to the elimination of its species. This wasn't the first time controversy tainted the fair. Back in 1872, a revered son of Groton, Col. Daniel Needham, had opened the fair with an address commending the town for gathering together each year, regardless of sex, party, or religious faith. What followed, however, was an event that sparked letters to the editor for weeks. Dr. Norman Smith, director of the Glee Club, proposed that the Cornet Band and his singers entertain the fairgoers with rousing campaign songs in favor of Republican candidate for reelection President U.S. Grant. Col. Needham determined that the Glee Club was at liberty to sing whatever they saw fit. An editorial in *Times Free Press* describes what occurred:

> *Thus the hall was set rolling, and afterwards the character of the meeting resembled a political gathering more than an agricultural fair. The Glee Club sang one Grant song after another till the end of the entertainment. It is true their leader offered to sing a Greeley song, if only one would come forward, but none was presented, either because there were no liberals there, or because they did not think that the proper time or place to have their cause promoted in that way, or because they had not expected the fair to be turned into a political meeting, and hence came unprepared to furnish campaign songs at such short notice.*

The Rev. John Badcock, emboldened by the partisan songs, took the opportunity to preach on Unitarianism. The editorial writer goes on to admit he is a Republican and liberal in his religion, yet he "think[s] it an outrage to drag religion and politics into a meeting of the people on the occasion of a town fair." The words went unheeded, for 60 years later, thanks to a movement founded to ensure a purity of genes and ideas, steeped in a fear of the new,

Groton lost its charming ancient agricultural fair filled with horses and cows, pigs and chickens, quilts and flowers, Catholics and Protestants.

LEFT: The front page of Thomas Dixon Jr.'s *The Clansman: An Historical Romance of the Ku Klux Klan*, published in 1905.

BELOW LEFT: Dr. H. W. Evans, Imperial Wizard of the KKK leading his Knights of the Klan in the Washington DC parade published in September 13, 1926 (National Photo Company Collection, Library of Congress).

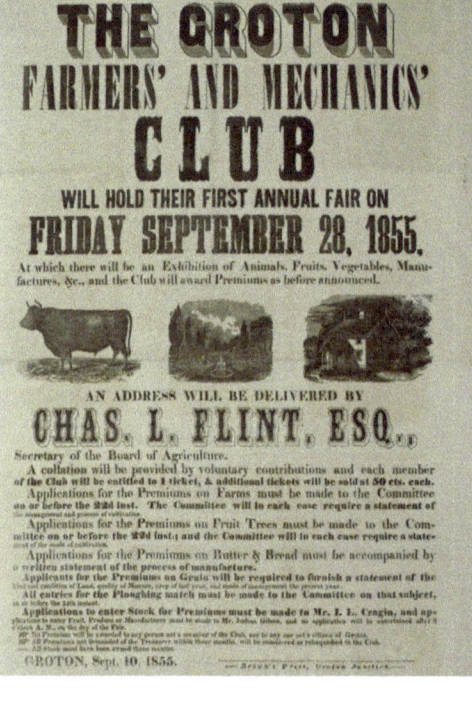

ABOVE: KKK gathering in 1924 (National Photo Company Collection, Library of Congress).

BELOW: The burning of an 80-foot cross, location unknown, August 9, 1925 (National Photo Company Collection, Library of Congress).

CHAPTER 8

MR. DANIELSON COMES TO GROTON

THE NEXT MR. DEERING

In October of 1916, workmen from Boston were seen placing loads of furnishings in an old house located at a crest of low hills near Groton School. This was the arrival of Richard Ely Danielson and his wife, Barbara Deering Danielson, who would next make their mark on Gibbet Hill. They had spent the summer making extensive repairs and improvements to the brick mansion whose grounds had been laid out by the architect of Boston's Emerald Necklace, Frederick Law Olmsted. The family also bought the Bowen Barker Place and kept the foreman on to run the farm and orchards. His total acreage neared 350, a sizable farm for New England, and had hundreds of productive apple trees spaced evenly in stonewalled grass fields. Groton and its hills, fields, swamps, and orchards would inspire them to buy more land over the years including the stone castle on Gibbet Hill in 1931. Even though the Danielsons would come to own property in Miami, New York, Chicago, and Boston, they considered Groton their home and Richard would die there in 1957 and be buried in the same cemetery as William Amos Bancroft.

The Danielson family had settled in America sometime in the late 1600s. James Danielson, a Scotsman, purchased land on Block Island, Rhode Island and then promptly joined up to fight Indians and was granted land in Connecticut for his pains. He went on to become one of the most influential men in the area with thousands of acres of land. The family garrison was located in present day Killingley. The societal position of the Danielson clan never wavered and is solidly prominent and substantial in the way only an old, old Yankee family can be. It remained that way for over two hundred years, remarkable for its loyalty to its tradition and histories. Richard's family boasted revolutionary era officers and plenty of capital. Richard's middle name and Grandmother's last name was Ely, another preeminent Yankee line. He was as noble and well bred as one can be in a democratic republic.

R.E. Danielson had been an English teacher at Groton School from 1907 to 1910. Although it was a prestigious position, the job did not pay very well. He left Groton in 1910 and journeyed to Chicago's booming financial markets seeking his fortune. Danielson's real gift was his polished Yale style and stunning good looks. Dick Danielson was a twin to Hollywood actor William Powell of *The Thin Man* movies, with his custom-made fedora and roguish charm. The wife he brought back from Chicago had more money than Nora Charles. Barbara Deering was a member of THE farm machinery dynasty—one of the richest families in America. Richard became the next Mr. Deering.

In 1957, Barbara's sister Marion made the top 20 list of the wealthiest of the inherited wealthy. The exclusive club included J. Paul Getty as #1, the Mellons at spots 2 through 5, John D. Rockefeller Jr. at 6, and various Duponts at 7, 8, 12, and 13. Number 10 was Howard Hughes, 11 was an Astor, 14 was Mrs. Edsel Ford, and Doris Duke of *Reader's Digest* fame was 15.

Olde Groton Days

Richard Danielson was 22 years old when he accepted the job at the Episcopalian Groton School, which had opened in 1884 and been presided over by Rector Endicott Peabody ever since; landing a position there was not a bad place to start any career. President Theodore Roosevelt was a frequent visitor and was related to the Peabodys through his daughter Alice. Rector Peabody went on to officiate at the wedding of Franklin Delano Roosevelt and Eleanor Roosevelt. The generous Lawrence family of Groton had donated the land for the school, once again, and the farm location was walked over and approved by America's first landscape architect, Frederick Law Olmsted, architect of Boston's public park system. Danielson's direct supervisor would be William Amory Gardner, the distinguished Greek scholar from Harvard and co-founder of the school with Sherrard Billings and Endicott Peabody.

Why the three young founders imagined they could start a private preparatory school is a mystery. 'Cotty' Peabody had started his working life as an investment banker with his father, Samuel Endicott Peabody, a partner at J.S. Morgan's company, the father of J. Pierpont. Billings and Peabody were not quite 27. Gardner was much younger. Only Billings had any teaching experience and that was only one year at a boarding school in northern New York. But somehow, their school worked like the fabled alchemist's formula for gold. By the time Peabody retired well into his 80s, Groton was the richest endowed private school and, arguably, the most respected in America.

By today's standards, Groton School and its Victorian "muscular Christianity" of the turn of the century was more like a reform school than an exclusive academy. Luxury had not yet become America's primary export fashioned by advertising executives. Peabody had been educated in England and adopted the English public school ideals of discipline and deprivation as the path to leadership. His boys were occupied every minute of the day, as idleness would certainly lead to trouble. They woke to a bell and ate to a bell and lined up to shake hands each evening with the rector and his wife before turning in to their spartan bedrooms, really just closet-like recesses along a long hallway, with only curtains for doors. They took cold showers each morning and exercised twice a day, but no one was asked to do any menial floor cleaning or bed making. Football was king and rowing was second and art and music were nonexistent.

Rector Peabody was straight-laced and proselytized his rigid values at every opportunity. He was a magnificently physical man and had trouble understanding boys who were not. His will-power and personal discipline were without contempt, however. He ruled with an iron hand but treated each boy as his own son and he was almost universally adored by all who came into his world—or, at least, deeply respected.

The second of the three Groton founders, the able Sherrard Billings, was called upon to fill in whenever the headmaster was away on sabbatical. Like Endicott Peabody, Billings was an ordained Episcopal minister and could therefore conduct chapel services. In fact, most who knew him considered him a much more gifted preacher than the rector. Relatively colorless when compared to his fellow founders, Billings was a conformist intensely loyal to the school and Peabody—a nerd without the temptation of intellectual wanderings. He waited to marry until he was almost 50 years old and sadly lost his wife to childbirth and his daughter a few years later. Billings was always a faithful servant, plodding along year after year, secure in his devotion to his savior and the deep love of his students.

And into the founding triangle is drawn a highly unlikely corner in the man of 20-year-old William Amory Gardner. He was Peabody's third choice after Teddy Roosevelt (who opted to go out west after the death of his first wife who was a cousin of Peabody) and Joseph Gardner, brother of William. "Wag" or "Billy Wag", as Gardner was known, was the opposite hypotenuse to Peabody's and Billings' right angles. He was a classically trained bohemian. He built a complex he called the "Pleasure Dome" near the campus, where beautiful Groton boys could swim, tell jokes on the stage, or play a game of squash while Billy sat beaming in the corner knitting a scarlet, green, and yellow sock. On Sunday afternoons he would serve up a sweet, two-colored concoction known as "Google" and a rock-hard stick of candy known as "blackjack". I wonder if these boys got the jest, or if Peabody even saw it. Greek life was, to Gardner, the good life.

An amazing story, which is too interesting not to repeat here, comes from Frank Ashburn's *Peabody of Groton*. This was a recollection of a graduate who may or may not have been present at the school's Hundred House when this event occurred. An unnamed boy was delegated to escort a prominent minister who came to the school to preach on a very cold day in winter. The boy knocked on Wag's door, and hearing voices inside went in and called to Mr. G.

They were beckoned up the stairs.

They started down the hall for the stairs. The voice went on. The voice continued excitedly, "It makes not the slightest difference that you won the first rubber, my dear boy", it said, "of course you did. That is la courtoisie de la maison. But the laurels of the evening, you must admit, belong to us. To be sure, in that first rubber we lost a few paltry farthings, whereas you, my poor fellow, owe me several lakhs and a crow of rupees."

"Further," it said, "while it pains me to wound a beloved disciple, I must point out to you, Bertie, that by your unfortunate error on the second hand in the third rubber you forfeited your membership in the Jockey Club of Constantinople and furthermore made our winning so overwhelmingly almost the equivalent of shooting sitting cows with a machine gun. Further still—well upon my word!"

His discourse was interrupted by the callers entering the bedroom. Standing before the fire naked as he was born except for a voluptuous pair of fur bedroom slippers, toasting his stern and stirring a large plate of porridge as he talked was Billy Wag himself. Holding more porridge and unsmiling in a morning coat was his butler and stretched out on the sofa, with even less on than Wag was Bertie [a former student].

" This is Dr.—" said the boy as solemnly as he could.

"Of course it is" said Wag, dropping an elaborate curtsy without spilling the porridge. "How good of you to come. This is Bertie, Dr.— one of our alumni. You find us a trifle informal my dear Sir, but if you will give us a moment until we finish our breakfast, perhaps I can persuade Bertie to put on some clothes more suitable for the day. Do be seated."

"I think I'd better get back, Sir," said the boy.

Mr. G bowed low. "If you will stay and converse I will gladly move over and share the fire with you. I cannot offer it all to you because only my rear is toasted and the front must be warm too this bitter day," he said, "if not, will you convey my respects to the Headmaster and tell him that all Groton boys should be made to learn to play bridge."

I wonder if Dr.— thought he had come across a lesson in the rules for strip bridge.

Wag was the definition of privilege and, after his father committed suicide, he and his two brothers were raised by their Uncle Jack Gardner and Aunt Isabella Steward Gardner. Around their dinner table in fashionable Back Bay might be Henry Adams, Henry James, John Singer Sargent, Charles Eliot Norton, James MacNeil Whistler, Edith Wharton, Anders Zorn, or Julia Ward Howe author of "Battle Hymn of the Republic", though not all on the same night. Oscar Wilde, while in Boston, was the guest of neighbor Julia Ward Howe. And many of Aunt Isabella's friends were gay— a great relief to what might have been a very confusing adolescence for William and his brother. What better examples than John Singer Sargent and Henry James for the queer life?

How did straightlaced Endicott Peabody get on with this vivacious young man? Amazingly, their relationship seemed a balanced one. It lasted until William Amory died in 1930. Peabody had sense enough to value humor and intelligence and, most importantly, loyalty, and if he felt irritation at Wag's role of devil's advocate, he understood how much he would benefit from such an honest point of view. Where the Rector was a robust athlete, riding a horse most every day and taking his bike to chapel, Wag preferred to go below on his yacht, the America's Cup defender *Mayflower*, as the excitement during a race was far too much for his delicate nature.

Gardner's views on teaching were documented in his many letters to the headmaster:

Let the best men, if they are to teach physics and chemistry, be men who know a good deal about Homer, Beethoven, Dante, and Velázquez. If they are to teach classics and history, let them know something of business, trigonometry, how long it takes a hen's egg to hatch … Also in longer deeper discussions always give the boy the reasons which convince you of the truth of a matter of religion or ethics. They may be a bit over his head … but the gain is great, I believe, in the long run. Anyone can tell the difference between black and white … a sensitiveness to the difference between light gray and just not quite so light gray can be inculcated in the classroom … The fundamental stimulant for the boy should be the desire to equip himself to give. He works that he may be a useful citizen, instead of a consumer; that his tools may be sharp for service, not blunt and useless.

These notions may seem commonplace to us today but they were revolutionary ideas in the 1880s.

Some of the struggle Gardner must have felt as someone diverging from the Puritan ideal of the strong, heterosexual male is revealed in an undated letter to Peabody. Gardner was a man whose time would not come for another hundred years. In an era when roles and responsibilities were fixed by moral convention, he had the courage (and means) to seek the actual truth of his being while he seriously contemplated how best to help his students understand their inner lives— which was, in his opinion, the most valuable life lesson.

My dear Cottie, don't ask me to talk in Chapel. It isn't in my line at all. I do my preaching daily in class—often out of season perhaps, but that is where it comes to me spontaneously, and when it is real and therefore of some use. Speaking on a set occasion whether at a dinner or elsewhere is simply misery to me and I don't feel real at all. Of course if the afflatus does blow in the course of the autumn I will tell you.

I love the school just as much as ever, but in some ways I positively disapprove of it. It is a complex thing I can't express clearly. If I found myself disloyal I should of course have to withdraw and I sometimes am worried by doubts on this point; but I still feel that as long as I heartily believe in the Christian Religion, in Purity, and in Social Service, my private views as to the morality or wisdom of the details of leading the boys to the desired end are not vital. But they would of necessity colour anything I might write for publication. Simply eulogy would simply not be true—where I am out of sympathy with the whole codes and systems I can work off my views at Faculty coffee; but in a book it would do harm or cause sorrow. I sometimes think you don't quite appreciate as being other than queer some of the standards I hold, because I say such queer and immoderate things. Unluckily a good many little things are to me symptoms of fundamentals. I talk of the symptoms, but that is because I have lain awake nights over the symbolized fundamentals.

This was the man to whom Richard Danielson reported in that first teaching job. He must surely have admired the unrelenting panache of William Amory's life. One of his favorite stories is how Wag, after his canoe was swamped in the Nashua River, "emerge(d) paddling with one hand and with the other still holding his volume of Sophocles before his eyes, while a drenched cigarette still dangled from his lips." How much Danielson learned about classroom discipline, however, is questionable. In the rigid environment of Groton, Wag was unique. He rarely corrected the boys' grammar in Greek and spent most classes digressing on any subject which captured his attention. One graduate remembers how the master came across a passage in the *Iliad* on dogs which led to a discussion of architecture in Belgium, the canals of Holland and New York State, various methods of burying the dead, famous epitaphs, the battle of Thermopylae, Aegean steamers, and the unreasonableness of publishers. As the students left the room, he chanted in Greek the lesson for the next day. What Danielson learned about life, however, must have been remarkable.

Wag's bond to Groton was strengthened by the caliber of men on the faculty. What a delicious life for an intellectual, enjoying the constant companionship of other extraordinary scholars. As early as 1895 Gardner donated part of his salary to increase the amount paid to young masters with the intention of keeping them at the school for their whole careers and stopping the traditional loss of talent to institutions of higher learning. Gardner's regard for Danielson is also documented. In 1908 he donated $3,000 and a house to help persuade masters who wanted to marry that they might move from the dormitories to domesticity at Groton for their life's work. " ... never let that issue be the cause of the loss of the right men, Danielson, Regan, etc. etc. whom we must keep."

It was natural, then, that when Danielson, his wife and two children returned to Groton in 1916, they bought the Joy estate from William Amory Gardner.

To Chicago and Back

Danielson writes about his travels up until his marriage to Barbara Deering in the second volume of the Yale Class of 1907. Here we see that the droll, falsely modest style of writing that would characterize his later career is already in place.

After the glooms of graduation I assisted at the joyous nuptials of Sam Morse. Recuperating in a few days, I left for Southampton, L. I., and spent a pleasant summer in the minimal labor of tutoring a young schollard. The following fall I went to Groton School, where for three years I deceived the authorities into a belief that I was a master of English literature. These years were very happy ones, as I found the life and work congenial. In the summer of 1908 I went to England and Scotland, and in the extreme north of the latter country I acquired no little fame on the moors as a dead shot, killing in two weeks' continual fusillading, one grouse, three ferrets, five dogs and eight or ten Scotsmen. The summer of 1909 I spent cruising on the Maine Coast, acquiring much nautical phraseology, a slight aroma of tar, and the sublime discovery of the Danielson cocktail. During these years I exercised what our secretary flatteringly describes as my "budding brain" in acquiring an M.A. from Yale in absence—and in the composition of a few stories of high life seen in a high light, which received the well-merited abuse of all my friends. The summer of 1910 I answered the call of the wild and came to Chicago, first stopping in New Haven for the Triennial, in the company of Class Dinosaur, Heath Woolsey. I came to Chicago, led by the lure of gold, and became a bond slave in the house of H. T. Holt & Company. My occupation consisted chiefly of pounding the resilient asphalt while stalking the elusive investor. Many of these investors were crude men who had learned in early youth how to say No! In October 1910, I accepted the position of assistant manager of the bond department of the Central Trust Company of Illinois, in which position I am still exercising my ingenious imagination. I was married on November 5, 1910, since which time the constantly decreasing little band of bachelors in our class, representing the survival of the unfittest, have received my profoundist pity.

The year 1910 was one of major transitions for Danielson. He left Groton in the spring, began work at the municipal, railroad, and corporation bond firm of H. T Holtz & Company on La Salle Street in Chicago, became engaged to Barbara Deering in late summer and switched jobs, working for Central Trust Company of Illinois in October, and was married by November 5th.

Not Paul Revere

As assistant manager of the bonds department at Central Trust, a general banking and trust business, Danielson soon had his name on the masthead with 25 others including the president and founder, Charles Gates Dawes. The name "Dawes" should be familiar to any American high school graduate who paid attention as it appears twice in every high school history book. Descended from founding stock, his father had risen to the rank of brevet brigadier general in the Civil War. His uncle gave his life in the same war. A distant grandfather, William Dawes, came to America in 1628 and his great grandson rode with Paul Revere on April 18, 1775, when he famously carried news at midnight that the British were approaching. Had Longfellow wanted a rhyme for "cause" instead of "hear" we might know more about this freedom rider.

Dawes took a different route that night from the one assigned to Paul Revere, which was supposed to ensure that at least one would make it to Lexington. Both arrived safely but it was a third companion, Dr. Samuel Prescott, joining them in Lexington, who made it to Concord. Revere was arrested but Dawes escaped back to Lexington. In his honor, reprinted here is a tribute penned by Helen F. Moore published in Century Magazine in 1896.

The Midnight Ride of William Dawes

I am a wandering, bitter shade,
Never of me was a hero made;
Poets have never sung my praise,
Nobody crowned my brow with bays;
And if you ask me the fatal cause,
I answer only, "My name was Dawes"

'Tis all very well for the children to hear
Of the midnight ride of Paul Revere;
But why should my name be quite forgot,
Who rode as boldly and well, God wot?
Why should I ask? The reason is clear —
My name was Dawes and his Revere.

When the lights from the old North Church flashed out,
Paul Revere was waiting about,
But I was already on my way.
The shadows of night fell cold and gray
As I rode, with never a break or a pause;
But what was the use, when my name was Dawes!

History rings with his silvery name;
Closed to me are the portals of fame.
Had he been Dawes and I Revere,
No one had heard of him, I fear.
No one has heard of me because
He was Revere and I was Dawes.

Grandson Charles Dawes' contribution to history amazingly outdid his ancestor's. He became a financial scholar after earning degrees in civil engineering and law. He published a book in 1894 entitled

The Banking System Of The United States And Its Relation To The Money And Business Of The Country. Not allowing his knowledge to be wasted, he amassed a huge personal fortune, eventually controlling 28 gas and electric plants in 10 states.

In 1895, Dawes began his political career after meeting Mark Hanna and William McKinley and acting as a fundraiser for the latter's presidential campaign. In 1901 he was a candidate for the U.S. Senate when McKinley was assassinated. However, without McKinley's endorsement he was not able to win, and another Republican was elected. He then founded the Central Trust Company of Illinois and was its president until he entered World War I. He later served as vice-president under Calvin Coolidge from 1926–29. In 1925 he was awarded a Nobel Peace Prize for the "Dawes Plan" to stabilize the German post-war economy. Too bad it didn't work. Maybe Hitler would be unknown to us today.

The Tractor Deerings

Unlike the Danielsons' in Connecticut, the Deering wealth was nouveau riche. Barbara and Marion's grandfather, William Deering, grew up modestly in South Paris, Maine, the son of a woolen manufacturer. Young William had his heart set on becoming a doctor but was pressured by his father to work at their small woolen mill. William soon perfected the skill of wool sampling, moved up to buyer, and eventually bought the mill. To market his products, he bought a store in Portland, Maine, and offered for sale a full line of dry goods. In 1861, he moved his family to Portland so he could serve as the senior partner of his expanded business, Deering, Milliken and Company. Early in the next decade, he left Deering, Milliken, and Company to found Deering Harvester Company, soon to become one of the leading manufacturers of farm equipment in the United States.

Meanwhile, another tractor family was moving in the same direction on a collision course. Cyrus Hall McCormick began his rise to stardom by tinkering with his father's simple reaper in 1831 at the family smithy in Walnut Grove, Virginia. He sold a few farm implements that became the equipment of choice for area farmers. In a brilliant business move, he and his brother, Leander, decided to move and set up a shop on the north bank of the Chicago River, right in the middle of a farming boom on the plains of Illinois and Iowa. Chicago, with its railways and stockyards, provided ample transportation for his growing export business. His dependable reaper sold like cheap gingham dresses in the Sears and Roebuck catalog.

Cyrus Hall and Leander in rapid order accumulated a huge fortune but suffered a major setback in 1871 when the entire McCormick reaper works was destroyed in the Great Chicago Fire. Thankfully the safe with all the company records survived. After insurance settlements, Cyrus still suffered a personal loss of $600,000— astronomical for the time. However, a new factory was up and running by February of 1873.

Just after William Deering began manufacturing, the two McCormick brothers formed the McCormick Harvesting Machine Company in 1879. The race was on for control of the burgeoning farm machinery market. Deering manufactured many of the same implements as McCormick but added improvement after improvement. In 1902, under the direction of J.P. Morgan and Company, the two companies along with Plano Harvester Company; Milwaukee Harvester Company; and Warder, Bushnell, and Glessner Company merged to form the world's largest farm equipment business, International Harvester Company. Cyrus Hall McCormick Jr. was named president and William Deering's son Charles, Barbara's father, was named chairman of the board. James Deering, Charles' half-brother, served on the board and as vice-president of sales. In 1906 International Harvester unveiled its first production tractor.

Charles Deering was an interesting man, in spite of his inherited wealth, whose life was filled with contradictions. He started out the son of an ordinary middle-class family in South Paris, Maine, but as the fortune of his family changed, like his father before him, he was pressured into turning away from the life he desired. He graduated second in his class at the United States Naval Academy in 1873. He served as the personal escort of ex-President Ulysses S. Grant and Mrs. Grant during their tour of China and Japan in 1879. In 1881 he was compelled to resign from the Navy at his father's request to enter the farm tool business. Despite his reluctance, Charles was soon successfully leading a major American corporation.

Ships and boardrooms aside, few knew that Charles' true passion was painting. In the 1870s, while living in Paris, he began to study art and became friends with the likes of John Singer Sargent and the Swedish portrait artist, Anders Zorn, both favorites of Wag's Aunt Isabella Stewart Gardner. Sargent tried to convince Deering to make painting his life's work but strong ties to his family won out. Even when his energy was taken up by running International Harvester, Deering continued to sketch and paint for the rest of his life and devoted his leisure pursuits to mentoring young artists in whom he recognized talent. He did manage to return to Paris in 1893 and painted in the studio of Zorn for the season, gaining proficiency as a portrait painter.

Barbara was the fourth child of Charles Deering by his second wife, Marion Denison Whipple.

The Big War

Two babies soon arrived at the Danielsons' Chicago home—Richard E. Jr. on April 5, 1913 and James on May 4, 1915. Dad decided to move the family back to the idyllic setting of his bachelorhood, bucolic Groton, which brings us back to their arrival in town in 1916. He bought one of William Amory's houses (Wag owned dozens) and an apple orchard. With his wife's cavernous pockets his whole life could be treated as a hobby, with no concern about making any of it a financial success. He informed the Yale alumni office that he was now a farmer.

Danielson had been interested in history since early childhood, probably at the feet of returning Civil War neighbors. He was not an armchair soldier, however. When, on April 6, 1917, the Americans declared war on Germany, Richard Danielson wasted no time — he did his basic training and shipped overseas in September as a volunteer for the American Red Cross under Major Murphy. He had spent the previous year on an archaeological expedition to Central America and was in Santiago, Cuba, during the brief revolution and he was keen for more adventure. He arrived in France by late September and was put to work on the Western Front near Oeuilly working at one of hundreds of American canteens providing food, clothing, and chocolates to the troops in the trenches. Barbara was left at home with her two infant sons, albeit with plenty of help.

Barbara's sister, Marion, had married Chauncey McCormick of Baltimore in 1914. Charles Deering had initially objected to the engagement because Chauncey "did not take life seriously enough." While a student at Yale Chauncey, clothed in overalls, was sent one summer to his relatives in Chicago to learn the business, starting at the bottom as a "day laborer." He seemed to flounder around for years and was still unimpressive to the Deerings or the McCormicks. When, on June 22, the McCormicks had the audacity to announce an engagement to Marion Deering in Baltimore, the Deerings, to the embarrassment of Chauncey, denied it. The wedding did however take place in Paris at one of the homes of Uncle James Deering two weeks later, where Chauncey had been transferred to a "more responsible position." He was soon thrust into the ultimate character-building opportunity, affording him hours of responsibility training—Chauncey enlisted.

Chauncey Brooks McCormick signed up to serve as the Western Representative for the American Field Service in France. Americans had been helping France's war effort since war broke out in August of 1914. In 1910, an American hospital started by Paris expats became a focal point for the compassionate American colony. They donated money, equipment, and automobiles, and even offered their personal services. Anne Morgan, J. P. Morgan's daughter, joined the American Fund for French Wounded (AFFW) and served as the head of the civilian committee, one of the women's motor corps units. The AFFW represented 700 sub-committees that amassed supplies and dollars for the French war effort. Anne opened up her 17th century chateau in Blérancourt as a center for humanitarian aid. It is now the Musée National de la Coopération Franco–Américaine. Gertrude Stein fled Paris in 1914 but returned in 1916 to volunteer with AFFW.

Margaret Brown, famous as 'Unsinkable Molly' the Titanic survivor, established a relief station for French soldiers. Amelia Earhart was a nurse in a French Red Cross hospital. Edith Wharton, whose family owned two houses in Groton, led a committee for refugees and urged the United States to join the European war. Mrs. Catherine Bancroft De Haviland, daughter of General William Amos Bancroft who had built the castle on Gibbet Hill 10 years earlier, immediately set up a small hospital, an "ambulance", at her husband's estate in France and trained as a nurse. She is quoted in the *Boston Evening Transcript* of February 26, 1916, saying "Our ambulance has changed quarters but will go to end of war. We have 11 soldier's beds instead of 8, besides 9 officer's beds. I have a new man —a baby—poor thing. His left arm was torn off at the shoulder. Two fingers of his right hand are gone and he has a huge wound which goes almost to the elbow. His lips and face are burned. He can do nothing for himself. I had thought of stopping the ambulance. I cannot now. I must go on until the end."

Chauncey McCormick was well connected to the substantial American colony in Paris, moving discreetly in exclusive American and French circles and was an eyewitness to the horrors of the Western Front. He was also an ideal candidate to recruit volunteers back in Chicago. He worked at the offices of Morgan, Harjes, and Company, an American bank branch of J. P. Morgan in Paris.

H. Herman Harjes, the 39-year-old senior partner of Morgan Harjes, was the third American to organize an ambulance corps in 1914. Yale, Harvard, and Princeton and hundreds of organizations from across the states sent cars and men to drive them. The Dawes family of Chicago sent a car and two of their sons to do the driving. The McCormicks sent three ambulances. Four Ford ambulances, donated by J.P. Morgan, were sent from New York. Ironically Henry Ford was a pacifist and in 1916 sailed to Europe on the "Ford Peace Ship." His mission was widely ridiculed and deemed a failure.

Groton women organized an AFFW chapter by the autumn of 1915. They met in homes and church halls and made bandages, hospital garments, dressing gowns, night shirts, and socks. The ladies made 3,062 garments between October 1916 and March of 1919. The money for materials was raised by endless rummage sales, concerts, and private contributions.

By contrast, even before the United States entered the war officially, her financial barons were raking in huge profits. J.P Morgan was instrumental in financing $1.5 billion in Allied military purchases during World War I and in arranging $1.7 billion in reconstruction loans afterwards. Bethlehem Steel, steered by Charles Schwab, became one of the biggest and most profitable companies in the world. Within six months of the first shots fired in August 1914, the company received more than $50 million in orders from Britain and France, plus the largest order in Bethlehem's history—$135 million from the British navy for howitzers, naval guns, shrapnel, shells, and 20 submarines.

Danielson's contribution at the American Red Cross canteen might sound sedate and sentimentally patriotic, by contrast, but it was nothing of the sort. He probably did enjoy quite a few nights drinking in Paris cafés with his brother-in-law and other expats, but he spent a large portion of his time right on the Front. Another young American, Ernest Hemingway, decided to quit his job as an ambulance driver because it was too boring and far away from the action. He chose to sign up as an American Red Cross canteen worker. Serving coffee right in the middle of a battleground is a new twist on food service. Six days before his 19th birthday, Hemingway was hit in the leg by an artillery shell. He was in a Milan hospital for two months.

After six months in Europe, Danielson secured a commission as a first lieutenant of Infantry in the U.S. Army on April 12, 1918, and was attached to G-2, S.O.S., where he served as an intelligence officer at Nantes, France, until November 3. He was transferred to Bordeaux and appointed assistant chief of staff of G-2, Base Section 2. He was made captain on February 15, 1919 and was discharged honorably in France on May 17. That same night in Groton, the Oddfellows were showing a flick by Charlie Chaplin called *Shoulder Arms*, which was set in France during the war in the town hall theater.

American soldiers had been trickling back to Camp Devens in Ayer, Massachusetts, since April. Many of them had shipped out from the makeshift barracks in Ayer two years before. The land had once belonged to the town of Groton and was the site of the Nonacaicus farm of Major Simon Willard. Discharged Captain Danielson met his wife in Chicago and then journeyed to the seat of his family in Danielson, Connecticut alone. To this cradle of respectability he returned to rest without his immediate family after the trials of a horrible war. Barbara went back to Groton on July 1 and she busied herself sprucing up the farm. She sent her employee Frank MacPartland to driver's school so she would have a local chauffeur. Richard Danielson, after regaining his composure, returned to Groton to take up a 1920s sporting life.

ABOVE LEFT: Richard Ely Danielson, 1910. A Christmas gift to W. A. Gardner (Courtesy of Groton School).

ABOVE RIGHT: William Amory Gardner (Courtesy of Groton School).

BELOW: Groton School, 1903 (from *The Brickbuilder* Vol 12, no5 1903, p113, Library of Congress).

CHAPTER 9

THE GROTON HUNT

THE ROUGE FOX

In 1934, a curious note appeared in the débutante section of *Time Magazine*. It seemed like a Groton fox was not behaving, well, like a fox. All autumn, members of the Groton Hunt Club of Gibbet Hill had been dealing with a rouge which acted more like a raccoon. As soon as this fox was cornered he turned and rushed the dogs who promptly ran away in terror. He could have been tormenting the Groton Hunt for years—American hunt clubs do not kill the fox. The famous fox was written about in a book of amusing stories called *Pageant of Life*:

> *TALLY-HO! yoicks! the hunters were riding to the hounds, pink coats, the traditional caps, and all the ceremonious paraphernalia of the fox hunt. Then an outrageous thing happened, most unconventional.*
>
> *The Groton Hunt Club in Massachusetts was one of the most fashionable and aristocratic outfits in the country. Everything was according to form except one fox. That mean old fellow committed the ultimate faux pas fox pah. The hounds and the huntsmen were after him, but instead of letting himself get killed, according to the Yoicks tally-ho tradition, the fox came to bay at a stone wall. Whereupon he jumped on the back of the nearest hound and started biting and scratching. The hound howled. The other hounds turned tail and ran, with the fox chasing after them. Then, as the huntsmen came galloping up, old Mr. Fox sat down in the middle of the bridle path and yelped defiance at the horses and riders, pink coats and all. That was the end of the Groton Fox Hunt for the day. The huntsmen followed the dogs home and the fox slid away into the woods.*

Foxhunting

The Danielsons were members of the sporting branch of the leisure class, in particular the horsey twig. Their favorite horse activity, which included racing and showing, was fox-hunting. They first hunted with the ancient and venerable Norfolk Hunt under the mastership of Mr. Henry Vaughan. The Norfolk Hunt began as a drag hunt in Dedham, Massachusetts in 1895 and moved to Dover in 1903. In contrast to their cousins in England and Virginia, New England fox hunters don't hunt foxes, and instead hunt bags of scent, usually anise seeds.

British fox hunting, in which foxes were ripped to shreds, was begun in England about 200 years ago. Squires of the time were seeking a faster, more exciting quarry, so they abandoned bunnies and stags. The English countryside was crawling with red foxes, and after the elimination of natural predators, the aristocrats performed a vital service by restoring the balance of nature.

Foxhound breeders soon began a studbook to breed the ideal specimen with enough stamina, speed, nose, and cry all in a medium package. The Duke of Beaufort began keeping hound-breeding books as early as 1728. Ever since, men and women who could afford kennel masters and stable managers have debated the superior qualities of their favorite line of tri-colored dogs.

A foxhound is a supreme athlete. He is asked to work two or three days a week each seven-month season walking 15 to 30 miles to the meet and running as much as 10 to 15 miles while in pursuit during the hunt. Is it any wonder most only last five years? The dog hound (male) stands 23 to 24 inches at the shoulder and the bitch a few inches shorter. A pack can have as many as 40 dogs.

Five unique pack-types have emerged in Britain with characteristic English names: the Curre, the College Valley, the Cotley, the Dumfriesshire, and the Scarteen—a black-and-tan hound. Each of these packs is bred to best hunt the particular area of the British Isles they inhabit. The U.S. breeders developed an American hound best suited to the unique country and quarry in the States. This, of course, is the basis of yet another Anglo—American rivalry, with many American hunt clubs choosing to stick with the purebred English hound.

The English fox is the red fox (*Vulpes vulpes*). The northern United States does have a native red fox but the English red fox has spread to all the states east of the Mississippi thanks to significant importing from Europe. America also has the native gray fox (*Urocyon cinereoargenteus*). Red and gray foxes are distinct species and never inter-breed. They are enemies and in many areas compete for the same territory. The gray fox has a unique scent and experienced huntsmen can tell by the cry of the pack which species the dogs are trailing. Gray foxes live in a relatively small territory in woods thick with briars and pines. Their habit is to circle and run short, giving less sport to riders interested in galloping and jumping rails. The gray fox is one of only two canines that can climb trees. The other is the common raccoon dog (*Nyctereutes procyonoides*).

Native American red foxes are very similar in appearance to their British cousins but with less population density. As a consequence these foxes will run for miles while pursued and seldom "go to ground" or find a hole to hide in. American hunt clubs do not kill the red foxes they locate but instead actively try to increase the fox population. English hounds are trained as puppies with a weekly exercise of ripping into a live fox called "blooding" keeping them keen on running for miles. American hounds do not need this training to keep them inspired, so American fox hunting does not generally attract bad press from the ASPCA.

The horse, the second factor in the fox hunting equation, must carry a rider of on average 145 lb for four to five hours, three times a week for at least six months. Highly bred thoroughbred racehorses are of little use in the hunting fields, with their fine bones and unpredictable behavior. The fox-hunting horse must possess sturdy legs, stamina, and a reasonable temperament. What works best is a crossbred animal called a hunter, generally a thoroughbred stallion with a mare of a sturdy local breed, such as a Connemara, Morgan, or draft.

It must be apparent at this point that while horse racing may be the sport of kings, fox hunting is the sport of dukes, earls, and counts. Early in the 19th century writer Henry Hall Dixon recorded that Herefordshire could be hunted for £2,000 (that's U.S. $12,000 today) but that didn't include the cost of the stables, horse, and hounds. Hunter horses today can cost anywhere from $5,000 to $15,000 and Master Dixon had 12 of them. By the Victorian era few aristocrats could afford to keep private packs so the subscription pack was developed whereby local titled riders and friends could join the club for a yearly fee.

Few human activities follow as many rules as fox-hunting—except for possibly golf. There is proper dress, proper vocalizations, proper equipment, and proper behavior. There is a proper riding order: master of foxhounds and field master first, then ex-masters and masters from other hunts; gentlemen and ladies with colors, including the whippers-in and huntsman, with buttons, members, then visitors and guests with sponsors; juniors with colors, without colors; and bringing up the rear, the field secretary.

Masters of foxhounds are the ultimate authorities in the field and in the boardroom. The huntsman attends to the hounds with one or two assistant hound handlers called whippers-in, a field master leads the riders and an honorary secretary collects fees and keeps track of horses and riders in the field.

Formal attire is worn during the regular season and consists of a black frock or Melton coat with a canary or tattersall waistcoat (vest), a white shirt, a white stock tie, and a horizontal gold pin. The breeches are to be tan or buff and of twill, cord, or leather, but not white (white is worn by the dressage folks). Boots are black (so are gloves), without that brown top worn by jockeys. Tabs at the top are sewn in but not sewn down. Ladies and gentlemen wear a black velvet hunting cap.

The "pinks" associated with hunting-scene paintings are only worn by permission of the master. First, one is awarded buttons with club insignia to replace the buttons on the black frock coat. If one is a very loyal and bold member, the master will "award one's colors" and the member is "entitled" to change their uniform. Ladies sew the club colors on their black coat collars; the gentlemen switch to scarlet coats with the club colors on the collar, but they must be satisfied with only three buttons in front. Any master can have four, and a full-fronted five-buttoner is the sole domain of the hunt master or staff. If you are hunting with another club, the pinks must remain in your closet.

With all this etiquette, hunting might seem stiff. It is anything but. Most of the conventions were established long ago to ensure everyone arrived back at the barn in one piece. It is much easier to see a bright red coat at a gallop than a black one. (Something the British military must have missed!) Clubs do lighten up and switch to informal wear, known as ratcatcher, in the "cub" season preceding the opening meet and sometimes during the regular season. Informal clothing is not jeans and sneakers, however. The jacket can be tweed, the shirt colored, and the boots brown.

The rulebook is practical in nature. For instance, you are not allowed to slam into the horse in front of you and if your horse kicks, she must endure a big red bow on her behind. Always smile at the landowners and remove your sunglasses when addressing them directly. The landlord is always right. Pooper scoop after your horse. Take your trailer full of poop home with you and don't smoke around the hay. Don't jump a jump if you don't know how to jump and close the gate behind you. Say thank you to the hunt master, and his relatives, friends, and staff. After all, he may one day allow you to wear the fancy buttons.

The Groton Hunt

The most coveted prize in fox-hunting is not the fox; it is the initials "M.F.H." ("master of foxhounds") added after your signature. R.E. Danielson started organizing the Groton Hunt in 1921, and he served as its first master of foxhounds in 1922. The National Steeplechase and Hunt Association officially recognized the Groton club in 1923 and the Masters of Foxhounds Association recorded the land they hunted over in 1925.

The first hunt did not begin until the fall of 1922. The master of a new hunt has the task of convincing skeptical and sometimes hostile farmers to allow riders in formal clothing to gallop back and forth over their fields. Danielson was an excellent diplomat and soon had permission from landowners in Groton, Pepperell, Harvard, and Shirley. He writes in the local paper, "In almost every instance the request has been granted with the utmost courtesy and good nature, and I should like to take this opportunity publicly to thank the landowners who have accepted my assurance that their interests would be respected and safe-guarded and who have generously and kindly granted this unusual request." In his long-winded style, he goes on to explain to the public what they will be up to:

> Fox hunting of the English sort, that is, following fox hounds on horseback was introduced into this country in the eighteenth century and has been steadily carried on ever since, especially in the south and more particularly in Virginia and Maryland. Pennsylvania and New York have also maintained a number of hunts for many years, and of late the sport has spread all over the country and is constantly increasing in popularity. Massachusetts has never seen a great deal of this kind of fox hunting, the nature of the countryside, the hills, woods, and swamps making it difficult, if not impracticable to ride a horse across country. In addition barbed wire has to large measure replaced the stonewalls and rail fences of our grandfathers. Two old established hunt clubs, Myopia at Hamilton and Norfolk at Medfield, have maintained for many years a high standard of hunting and Mr. Higginson at Lincoln and Harry Smith at Worcester

have kept famous packs of hounds until recently. There is, at present, no recognized pack of hounds in Middlesex County. It occurred to the writer, who prefers fox hunting to any other form of sport, that it might be possible to get together a few fox hounds as an experiment and offer an opportunity to the people of the locality to take up a sport which has proven so enjoyable and so valuable elsewhere.

There are two kinds of fox hunting or "riding to hounds," actual fox hunting and so-called "drag hunting." The first in so rugged a country as ours consists mostly of spending a number of hours on horseback, riding up and down wooded roads and around wood lots, trying to hear the far-off cry of the hounds as they follow one of the rare foxes which has escaped the snare of the trapper. The odds are all on the foxes, and the hounds, who are stout and fast enough to run down a native wild fox before he can take refuge under ground, are few and far between.

Drag hunting is really an imitation, an illusion of what fox hunting would be if the country were all together suitable. A good line of country is selected, giving a run of from three to twelve or fifteen miles free from wire and swamps, and over this country, fields, fences and walls a mounted man rides, dragging after him a bag containing fox litter, reinforced with oil of anise seeds. Some time later the hounds are thrown in on this line of scent which they follow at great speed, followed in their turn by the huntsman, the whips and the members of the "field." It is not hunting, but is certainly the most vigorous, exciting, and stirring form of horseback riding which is possible in this part of the world.

In most instances hunting of this kind is carried on by established clubs, the members of which subscribe to pay the expenses of keeping the hounds, etc. In this case the thing is an experiment. No club is organized or contemplated. The hounds are owned by the writer who is entirely willing to maintain them until such time as it may seem desirable either to give them up or change the system. Any resident of Groton or the adjacent towns, who has a horse that will gallop and jump an ordinary wall, will be very heartily welcome to ride with us, provided that he or she will conform to the discipline necessary to protect the interests of the landowners; the expense of hunting to such persons, beyond the upkeep of their horse will be nothing at all.

The group began riding to scented bags on Saturday, September 16, 1922. Notices in the paper announced that the drag hounds could be followed every Monday and Saturday and the foxhounds would be chased on Wednesdays. An average of 15 or 20 mounted enthusiasts from Boston, Fitchburg, Groton and surrounding towns turned out that fall for each meet following over 30 baying hounds. Mr. Danielson presided over the drag course but he deferred to the wisdom of Fred Armstrong as the huntsman when it came to managing the hounds after real foxes. The whips were Michael Maroney and Mrs. Danielson who rode exclusively in a sidesaddle.

In this first year, the hunt met at various locations. For the fox and drag hunt, typical starting points were the Woods Village in Shirley, the Lowthorpe School at the Low Estate in Groton, Groton School, Groton Inn, and various farms from Harvard to Pepperell. Announcements were made each week in the local papers.

In the fall of 1923, the *Boston Evening Transcript* published an article praising Mr. Danielson and his hunt. "The difficulty in starting a new hunt," the article goes on to say, "lies in proving that it is a benefit, not a nuisance." With the popularity of the hunt came a new flow of wealthy outside leisure-class money. The close of the hunt season in 1922 saw an "immediate rise in real estate values and a demand for places...three large estates near Groton were sold at values entirely improbable if the attraction of the hunt had not existed."

Another beneficiary was horse dealer Peter T. Roche of Leominster who recognized an opportunity when he saw it. He organized the Groton Hunt Stables where he kept 28 hunters, some owned privately but most made available for let to persons unwilling or unable to keep their own. The Inn also jumped at the chance to cater for the Hunt. At the time, the Groton Inn was widely known for excellent cuisine served in a fine atmosphere of lovely china and starched linen. Out-of-town guests did not hesitate to hire a room for the night after a day of "capping."

Although the hunts were still technically free to the public, Danielson did start accepting voluntary subscriptions for his pack of English hounds acquired from the American established packs of Chagrin Valley, Cheshire hounds, and W. Plunkett Steward. Danielson claimed that the virtues of the American hound of "individuality, nose, and voice were wasted in a drag pack." The hounds stayed at his newly completed modern kennels about a half-mile from his house on Joy Lane.

The Danielsons' personal barn at their home on Joy Lane would stable many great hunters. One of his horses, Waynefleet, was purchased in the fall of 1916 and Dick Danielson carried a picture of him and his wife's horse Baby Bennett (along with his wife and children) in his wallet while he was away in Europe during World War I. Another beloved steed went by the name of Banbury Cross, and was ridden to hounds by the Danielson huntsman and groom, Fred Armstrong. (Three of the four Danielson grooms were named Fred, the other two being Fred Hosmer and Fred Lovejoy. The fourth was a man named Mr. Roberts from Littleton.) Banbury was "an excellent hunter but the sloppiest jumper," writes Danielson in his book *Martha Doyle and Other Sporting Memories*. He had a bad habit of running through his jumps instead of over them and was believed to have iron legs.

The second year was limited to drag meets held every Wednesday and Saturday starting at 8 o'clock in the morning during the month of October. The course varied a bit but was on average a five mile fast ride featuring jumps over stone walls from four to five feet (larger than today's standard), with an occasional "in and out" or a "post and rail." When the weather became colder in November and the horses were fitter, the runs lengthened to 10 or 12 miles. The Groton Hunt chose to honor the Continental Army when it selected patriotic dark blue coats with brass buttons and buff collars as its colors instead of the traditional "pinks." This American hunt club did not ride in English redcoats.

The hunt was soon a huge success. Groton real estate values rose as other members of the hunt fell in love with Groton and bought estates. The Danielsons began in earnest to breed their own pack of hounds and in May of 1925, 150 invited guests came to see the new puppies. The dogs were shown at hunting trials and brought back many ribbons and championship cups. Dick Danielson, working with Mr. Vaughn and Mr. Appleton, masters of the Norfolk and Myopia hunts respectively, started the first New England Hunts Hound Trials in 1922.

The Groton Farmers and Mechanics Fair, which was still running at this point, seemed a natural venue for Danielson's interests. He introduced the Groton Challenge Cup and it attracted expert riders from all over New England. *The Herald* boasted that since 1885 only the Brockton Fair could compare with the Groton Horse Show, held for two days in late September. Danielson was elected vice-president of the Fair in 1925 and soon the entire Horse Show committee was made up of Groton Hunt members. The Fair grew to a three-day event and by 1927 featured a seven-piece orchestra, boxing, dancing, a dog show, and horse racing, both flat track and harness. The following year almost 10,000 people attended the Friday night horse show, many times the population of the town. The Groton Hunt Challenge Cup was won by a team made up of

R.E. Danielson on Martha Doyle, George Timmins on Glenorky, and Philip Wharton* on Submarine.

Danielson's favorite horse, Martha Doyle, was immortalized in a short story of the same name in *The Atlantic Monthly*, which became the lead story in and title for a collection of sporting stories he published in 1938. She had been bought by Peter Roche as a two-year-old and discovered by Mrs. Danielson at a show in Worcester, where Martha won the high jumping event by flinging herself six feet four inches into the air. Barbara bought the young horse on the spot and later gave Martha to her husband as a birthday present. Forever grateful to him for finding Martha, the Danielsons gave Peter Roche the nod when the Groton Hunt needed a stable manager.

Martha was a big (16.2 hands) brown thoroughbred with an alpha mare mentality—she had to take the lead. In fact, Richard always claimed Martha's predilection for speed was the reason he started the Groton Hunt. Not being a master, he could not lead in the Norfolk Hunt and therefore had to spend the entire day hauling back on her reins. Martha was hunted twice a week for 11 years and only dumped Danielson twice. It took two pages in his book explaining how this was his fault not hers. Martha is buried in the horse cemetery on the Danielsons' estate beside the Nashua River.

Beginning in 1928, the reorganized hunt moved their

---

* Philip Wharton grew up in Groton at the Elms on Pleasant Street. He was the son of William Fisher Wharton, assistant secretary of state under President Harrison, and Susan Carberry Lay. William F. Wharton had a son by his first wife, Fanny Pickman, named William Pickman Wharton. William P. lived in Groton at Five Oaks on Broadmeadow Road and was a prominent conservationist who was instrumental in the success of the National Park system along with Teddy Roosevelt and Frederick Law Olmstead. He served as President of the National Park Association from 1935 to 1953. William F. Wharton's brother was Edward Robbins Wharton, the husband of novelist Edith Wharton.

headquarters to the estate of James Lawrence* in Farmer's Row. The colonial "Lawrence Homestead" had been enlarged by 1876 by John Hubbard Sturgis and had recently undergone further renovation. On June 16th, the Groton Hunt Club opened their season with a big party at the Lawrence Estate. A large audience gathered at 4:30 p.m. for an indoor tea, unable to enjoy the lovely gardens due to rainy weather, followed by dinner at Danielson's home. Piling back into cars, the boisterous group danced until midnight in the large ballroom designed by Sturgis 40 years before. The fireworks display scheduled for 9 p.m. was impossible because the storm had intensified, while later sleeping residents of Groton sprang out of bed at 11:45 p.m., thinking the world was coming to an end. The downpour had subsided enough that the inebriated flappers thought it was a good idea to shoot off the fireworks, forgetting it was way past a farming community's bedtime.

The Groton Hunt began to rent the buildings on Gibbet Hill that had formerly been used by the Groton Private Hospital and owned by Albert Phelps. They used the facility for most of their events including the formal Annual Hunt Club Ball in the late 20s. Evening dress and plenty of food and drink were the standard. The temperance movement had saturated the valley and by 1903 the only legal beer between Boston and Templeton was in Shirley. Groton had been "dry" for many years so Prohibition was not much of a change. A little thing like a constitutional amendment did not deter the clubbers from letting the liquor flow.

The local landowners over whose fields the horsemen hunted

---

*   The earliest Lawrence ancestor to live in Groton was John Lawrence, who moved to town in 1662. His original homestead was on the site of the Gibbet Hill farmhouse on Lowell Road, for many years the home of Joseph F. Hall and later belonged to General William Amos Bancroft. John Lawrence was an original land-proprietor and the proud owner of a 20-acre right. It was burned by Algonquins.

were treated in October to a night of luscious food and live music with catchy titles like "Roll Another Log On the Fire" and "Shine On Harvest Moon." In 1928, a large tent was erected in the gardens of the Lawrence Homestead, and a banquet was catered by a firm from Nashua. Music was provided by an orchestra this time and locals sang, danced, and were awake for the fireworks display. The papers reported "feats of horsemanship and dog races were some of the attractions." The Pepperell town hall was another location for the event, where any liquor had to be in a pocket flask. One local resident remembers a year when a magician entertained the landowners. This show of good-will helped to cement a loving relationship between the townies and the hosts that lasted for over 20 years.

The Castle Burns

When the Ayer High School Class of 1930 asked to book the Hunt Club for a Fourth of July outing, the answer was yes. Agnes Cody was there that day and recalled that the students had a wonderful day until tragedy struck. A few kids had brought along a bag full of firecrackers with the intent of climbing up into the turret and letting them off. Somehow some old newspapers in the round room were set on fire and instead of stamping them out, the panicked children turned and ran down the circular stairs, afraid of getting in trouble.

Soon the glorious bungalow was on fire and fire trucks raced up the hill. The pumper truck hooked up to the hydrant and the men watched in horror as the water sputtered halfway up the tower wall. The Groton water reservoir was just over the hill and did not provide enough pressure to drive the water up 30 feet to the top, where it was needed. Soon sparks from the tower caught the roof shingles and finally the giant beams over the main house, and the town below watched from Main Street as the Bancroft castle became a roaring fireball. Water was pumped over the rest of the buildings and the surrounding foliage in hope of preventing the ignition of the entire hill. After hours of fighting the blaze, the firemen did prevent the destruction from reaching the other buildings in the complex, but the bungalow was reduced to a smoking mess of charred cross beams with a casing of steaming hot rocks. Nothing inside the castle was saved.

Mrs. Deering Buys Gibbet Hill

The Hunt Club's lease at the Lawrence Estate was due to end in 1931. It was imperative that the club find a new location. The club had been using the facilities from time to time as staging grounds for hound trials and hunts and enjoyed the lovely view. Barbara Danielson solved the problem by buying the 35 acres atop Gibbet Hill including the Bancroft bungalow ruins and all the former private hospital buildings. She leased the land and its building back to the Hunt.

A building committee consisted of iris enthusiast Robert S. Sturtevant, Mrs. George H. Timmins, Mrs. Gordon MacTavish, and Mrs. Frederic Dumaine, all of whom had summer homes in Groton. The hospital ward was gutted of its rooms. Cyprus paneling covered some walls and hardwood floors gleamed throughout. A wide staircase led to the rooms upstairs. The theater building was weatherproofed and shut up. Chairman Sturtevant put to work some of his students—he was director of the well-respected Lowthorpe School of Landscape Architecture* in Groton which was attended exclusively by young ladies from around the country. A new stable was planned for below the bungalow ruins, but was never built. The two old barns built in 1915 by Dr. Ayres were torn down—a large barn just off Hollis Street was used by the Hunt Club horses.

The annual Thanksgiving Day Hunt was established soon after. Mrs Stacey Benson, who lived on Farmer's Row and hunted for years, recalls that a group of about 30 riders would meet in the morning for

---

*   The Lowthorpe School, opened in 1901, offered one of the first courses in landscape architecture for women. The school was started by Judith Motley Low on her country estate in Groton.

drinks at the Groton Inn. They didn't have breakfast until after the hunt was over, usually about noon, so they must have needed the extra courage. After cocktails, the impeccably mounted spectacle clattered through town and out west toward the fairgrounds and the trail along the old rail bed. Groton historian Helen McCarthy Sawyer called the parade "one of most picturesque sights" she ever saw.

A fixture every year at the Thanksgiving Day Hunt was textile tycoon Frederic Christopher Dumaine. According to Groton Hunt member Roger Prouty,* Mr Dumaine was a colorful character, arriving at the hunt events in a stocking cap on a pinto horse named Pat Rooney. "In the high-collar areas of Boston, Frederic C. Dumaine flaunted an open-shirt background, cussed a blue streak, and walked with a bearlike roll," *Time Magazine* writes in 1948. Frederic started as an office boy at Amoskeag Mills, in Manchester, NH, and rose to take control of the mill, at one time the world's largest manufacturer of cotton cloth. He bought a mansion on Farmer's Row for his second wife, Louise, in 1927. Frederic left a lovely memorial to his foxhounds and favorite horse Pat Rooney on the grounds of his estate. Part of his land, renamed Groton Place, was eventually donated to the New England Forestry Foundation and is open to the public.

His daughter, Elizabeth, was also a member of the Thanksgiving Hunt and started the Nashoba Hunt, a reconstituted Groton Hunt after it had disbanded for a few years during World War II. She served as its master from 1951 to 1953. She had been joint master of the Golden Vale Hunt in County Wexford, Ireland, from 1949 to 1951. Betty was an unforgettable figure on a horse. She weighed in at over 350 lb. at the time of her death and must have ridden gigantic horses. Her roommate in school ended up becoming the mother of the king of Thailand and she made Betty the head of

---

*   Roger Prouty, born in 1920 in Littleton, MA was a Professor Emeritus of History at University of Mass Boston. Roger joined the Groton Hunt at age 16.

her foundation in the United States. Betty wrote a book about this relationship called *The Princess Mother*.

In 1929, the National Steeplechase and Hunt Association recognized 60 hunt clubs. In 2002, the word 'Hunt' was dropped from the organization. Hunt Clubs are now regulated by the Masters of Foxhounds Association, which has 50 clubs listed. Not bad in the era of the computer and automobile. Betty's legacy, the Nashoba Hunt, was reformed in 1964. The hunt barn moved to Pepperell, MA, one town east of Groton, and conducts drag hunts to this day.

TOP LEFT: English Foxhound in 1915.

TOP MIDDLE: American Foxhound in 1915.

ABOVE: Red Fox.

LEFT: Memorial bench at Groton Place (Photo by the author, 2009).

BELOW: The New England Hunt Hound Trials, hosted by the Groton Hunt Club, was begun at Kemp's Four Corners in Pepperell. Mrs. Danielson is seen in the foreground riding side saddle. She is the Whipper-in, controlling the hounds with her long whip. Behind her is Mr. Danielson. Wednesday November 4, 1931. (*Boston Evening Transcript*, Boston Athenæum).

ABOVE: The first hunt clubhouse on the Danielson property. Note the mounting block in the inset. The kennels were located nearby (Photo by the author, 2009).

BELOW: Over 50 riders gathered for the New England Hunt Hounds Trial hosted by The Groton Hunt in 1931 (Photo by Morton, *Boston Evening Transcript*, Boston Athenæum).

ABOVE: Fred Armstrong, Groton's Kennel Huntsman, holding champion hound, Traveler, in 1931. (*Boston Evening Transcript*, Boston Athenæum). Traveler, bred by the Danielsons, "was the best hound I've ever know," says Dick Danielson. He won the New England Hound Trials three times in a row from the pick of ten or eleven packs. In 1931, Traveler, competing in the Five-Mile Run after being judged best in the Best Cross-Bred Hound Dog in the morning show, stopped for a drink after gaining a 150-yard advantage. Refreshed, he crossed the finish line a nose ahead of Junior's Tip Toe, owned by Mrs. I. Tucker Burr.

LEFT: Fred Hosmer about 1986.

BELOW: Foxhound statue on the former Dumaine property, now a public park. A memorial to Frederic Dumaine and his horse Pat Rooney are nearby (Photo by the author, 2009).

BELOW: Banbury Cross, after having broken away from his hay rake, caught up to Fred Amrstrong as he was walking the hounds along Shirley Road (Illustration by Edwin Megargee, *Martha Doyle and Other Sporting Stories*).

ABOVE: The Groton Hunt Club Team winning the Nathaniel Thayer cup at the third annual fall meeting of the Norfolk Hunt Club at Medfield, MA Left to right: George H. Timmins*, John Parkinson Jr., Philip Wharton, Fred Grinnell, R.E. Danielson and Henry Vaughan, Master of Fox Hounds. Published in the Boston Herald on October 20, 1929 (Herald-Traveler Photo Morgue, Boston Public Library).

BELOW: The bungalow on fire, July 4, 1930 (Courtesy of Louise Naylor).

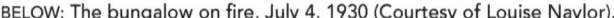

*   George Herbert Timmins, of Ware, MA, had a home in Groton on Farmer's Row. Beginning 1928, he was joint Master of the Groton Hunt Club with R.E. Danielson. Timmins fell of his horse while riding the hunt and died of a burst spleen a few hours later.

ABOVE: The Lawrence Estate, home of the Groton Hunt from 1928 to 1931 (Photo by the author, 2009).

BELOW: Closeup of the new clubhouse formerly part of the Groton Private Hospital complex (Photo by Morton, *Boston Evening Transcript*, Boston Athenæum).

Close-up of New Clubhouse, Formerly a Hospital Building   (Photo by Morton)

It's rare, today, to find
a pedigree completely
from one program.
We registered calves, this year,
that were 12th generation
of our own breeding.

Bill Conley

GIBBET
HILL
FARM

TO:

*Northeast Angus
Breeders*

CHAPTER 10

NOTHING BUT BLACK COWS

MISS MARION

Born in 1921, six years after her youngest brother and two years after her father had returned from World War I, Marion Danielson was more like an only child. Her brothers would be busy at Groton and Yale through the formative years of her childhood and her parents were busy with the Groton Hunt and *The Atlantic Monthly*, and other charitable and social events.

After Marion finished eighth grade, her folks sent her off to a horsey school in Middleburg, Virginia, called Foxcroft, where she did her duty academically and socially but gave up riding for good. Ultimately, Marion preferred life on the farm in Groton to wearing gowns of light-blue organza trimmed with silver beads and she was soon home to play with her animals.

Marion loved growing up on a farm. She rode the hunt with her parents but loved the cows more. From time to time, Barbara Danielson kept a few black baldies along with her dairy cows, fox-hunting horses, and dogs on the farm next to Groton School. Black baldies are beef cows produced by crossing a red-coated white-faced Hereford with an all black Angus. During World War II, Marion bought two steers to get around meat rationing, and after the family had eaten both, she bought a bull and four cows. Fascinated with breeding and genetics, Marion began to go to Townsend to buy purebred Black Angus cows. She started a lifelong habit of keeping detailed records. Soon her black cattle outnumbered her mother's. Mother suggested that perhaps Marion should have her own farm.

Marion enrolled at Vassar College the fall of 1940—the female equivalent to her family's Yale legacy. After she graduated, *The Washington Post* hired Marion to work in the editorial department. She would work in most phases of journalism for the rest of her life, though never as a writer. Answering the call of her country, she became a staff aid caseworker for the American Red Cross in Washington from 1944 to 1946. After the war ended, Marion's father gave her a job at *The Atlantic Monthly*, where she became a reader and editor honing her skills choosing manuscripts and shaping each issue. Her second husband Douglass Campbell later said of his wife: "Although she was not a writer herself, she was always interested in writing and enjoyed stimulating others to write."

Back in Groton, the home guard marched up and down Gibbet Hill over farmland owned by Joseph Connolly. They drilled to the top of the hill where the Groton Hunt had a clubhouse owned by Marion's mother. Although club activity stopped during the war because most of its members, including the Danielsons, were away fighting the Nazis.

Marion Buys Gibbet Hill Farm

Her love of black cows and her mother's annoyance at the space they occupied led Marion to purchase 200 acres of land, three barns, and a house from Joseph Connolly of Lowell Road on October 21, 1947. The farm was just below the tract owned by her mother. Joe was the son of Dennis Connolly, who had purchased the farm in October of 1919 from William A. Kemp and Frank R. Bennett ,who had picked it up at auction from General Bancroft in 1912. When Marion bought it, the place had been for sale for a couple of years, and was listed at $20,000.

In the years since Bancroft, the farm had been run as a dairy operation but had fallen on hard times and was in serious disrepair. The glorious Bancroft apple orchard was only a remnant. Marion paid only $18,500, pointing out she'd need to put money into the place. Joe Connolly immediately went out and bought a brand new 1948 Buick with the proceeds. He was still driving the car in 1960.

Half Moon Pond was a vernal (seasonal) wetland and Joe Connolly had been able to cut good hay from the fields with his horse. He stacked the hay loose in the huge truss barn, a common practice for generations. The fodder was removed with a hayfork as needed to keep the dairy cows through winter. The rough-hewn timbers cut from old-growth trees were thicker than a man's middle. Bill Conley, Marion's new farm manager, obtained permission to buy the first square baler in Groton and got to work turning the massive haystack into a wall of bales. The dusty haystack that had filled the barn to the rafters was soon reduced to a bit less than half the space.

Fenced pastures were needed before the Angus herd could be moved over from across town. Local men were hired and the job continued into a bad winter, forcing them to hack through ice on Half Moon Pond to set the posts. The men were paid $1 per day for hauling fence posts on toboggans and working in brutally cold conditions.

Starting with 10 cows, Gibbet Hill Farm built a small purebred Angus herd into one of the most famous in the world—in 1997, the farm achieved Historic Angus Herd status. The award honors members of the American Angus Association who have owned a herd for more than 50 years. Only about 100 herds have been recognized since 1988.

For Marion Danielson, late 1949 to 1950 was a life-changing year. She formed lasting bonds with two men who would stick with her until one of them died. The first, Malcolm Strachan, became her first husband and the father of her children, and the second was Bill Conley, the man who would become the de facto father of Gibbet Hill Farm.

To promote the new Angus farm, Marion and her farm staff put together a field day in October 1949 in the middle of her plans for her wedding, which would take place in New York a few months later. Over 200 breeders wanted to come to the event: a day of herding dog demonstrations, information sharing, bovine beauty pageants and, of course, beef eating. Bill Conley, a student in the University of Connecticut's animal science department with sheep dog experience and low expectations for compensation, accepted the field day job.

The next April, the newly graduated Bill received a letter offering him the position of managing the startup breeding operation. He was sorely tempted. He and Marion shared the same goals for the future of the Angus breed: a bigger, taller cow which calved with ease and whose progeny gained well. Also, as a Deering heir, Marion had the means to maintain goals through the vagrancies of beef cattle fashion. Marion's operation was a serious enterprise, not a hobby farm. But Bill had his heart set on attending grad school and he was newly married to the daughter of a dairyman who had seen enough cows for several lifetimes. Marion, the psychology major, convinced Bill to take the farm for a year or two appealing to his love of a challenge. Bill Conley managed the farm until Marion died in 1998.

The Aberdeen-Angus

Angus (in America) or Aberdeen-Angus (anywhere else in the world) is the only premium steak in America called for by name. Today an advertisement for a beef steer will most likely picture the compact, black, hornless Angus, replacing the image of the whiteface Hereford of 40 years ago.

The rugged little black cow came from the northeastern coastal region of Scotland in counties bearing the names Angus and Aberdeen. Some historians believe that hornless cattle are direct descendants of aboriginal cattle indigenous to the districts where they are still found. Likenesses of polled cattle are found in prehistoric carvings in the region. The family cow was the "black sleekie," "doddies," or "hummlie," distinguishing it from the black curly-haired polled Galloway.

Nicknames seem natural for an animal that is a close member of the family for half of the year. Celtic Britons lived in an ecosystem that necessitated their unique style of animal husbandry. The narrow valleys and sparse high country could sustain cattle in the summer, but were useless in the winter months. The docile cows were rounded up and tied in a barn with a rope long enough to allow each to lie down where it was standing. It takes an animal of extraordinary temperament to yield to that level of confinement while being fed a diet of large yellow turnips.

"Money, nothing more romantic or idealistic than that, brought the first Aberdeen-Angus to North America," writes M. R. Montgomery in his wonderfully entertaining book *A Cow's Life*. The first Angus were brought to America in the 1800s to satisfy a desire for beef meals at an inn. Until the mid-19th century, to eat a meal cooked by someone other than a relative was a misfortune.

In 1861, Sir George Simpson, governor of the Hudson's Bay Company, ordered two registered Angus (not Aberdeen, which had a separate registry in Scotland at the time) to be sent to his home in Canada. He received a cow named Dorothea and a bull named Orlando from the famous herd of the Earl of Southesk. The governor died shortly thereafter, before he had time to establish a permanent herd; nobody knows what happened to the prized pair, for they had absolutely no impact on the cattle in the area.

The next bulls imported into the United States had a more favorable fate. They were bred to rangy longhorn cows. George Grant, a Brit, formed Victoria Colony in central Kansas with the intent of attracting other wealthy English expats into the cattle business. Grant owed a big part of his fortune to Queen Victoria's greatest sadness. In 1861, her beloved husband, Prince Albert, contracted cholera caused by faulty drains at Buckingham Palace. Grant bought up all the black crepe in London and when the Prince finally died, Grant overcharged the grieving families, knowing full well they would not have the strength to object.

His four bulls arrived in Kansas in 1873 but the colony disbanded within five years after Grant's death and the bulls were sold. American cattlemen liked the hybrid vigor of the crossbred calves so much they ordered more from Scotland. Between 1878 and 1883 twelve hundred "doddies" arrived in the Midwest. Today the United States has forty times more registered Angus cattle than Britain.

William Brown, a native Scotsman who was hired to run the Ontario Experimental Farm, founded the first perpetuating herd of purebred Aberdeen-Angus. In 1876, a year old bull named Gladiolus arrived. He was joined the next year by a fetching cow named Eyebright, already pregnant when she arrived. Her calf, Eyebright 2nd, was the first purebred Aberdeen-Angus born in the New World. Gladiolus and Eyebright were successful in producing more offspring and with the addition of other purebred cattle in the next few years, a permanent herd was officially established. Eyebright 2nd was shipped to Kansas State College, making her the first purebred cow imported from Canada to the United States. Canada is the true origin of the Aberdeen-Angus in North America.

The Gibbet Hill Angus

By the time Bill Conley showed up for work in 1950, the Gibbet Hill Farm supported 30 head of cattle on 190 acres. Thirty-five years later he would be managing 1,200 acres with over 200 cows*, plus row crops, hay fields, apple orchards, and logging forests, the original farm having spread to many non-contiguous parcels all around Groton and surrounding towns. He would manage in those years with little interference from Marion Campbell, a business style she learned from her father at *The Atlantic Monthly*.

Marion Campbell and Bill Conley shared a vision for the Angus breed in America. Although it was respected by cattlemen for its hardiness and crossbreeding vigor, the Angus was still considered by many to be a toy for "gentlemen" ranchers. The Hereford was the standard of the day and had been bred to maximize beef traits: large muscular frames, gainability coupled with low birth weight, and ease of calving. Like their dogs, Victorian Englishmen bred the Angus stock into an oddity. The black sleekies had become a vain possession. It became fashionable to produce a bull so

---

*   At one time Gibbet Hill Farm had 600 cows.

stocky and short that his belly would nearly rub the ground as he waddled before the judges. A bull's ability to gain weight was valued more than his ability to produce offspring, a practice that was bound to fail.

The star of the herd was already munching grass when Conley inspected the farm for the very first time. Her name was Belle of Malden and Marion had picked her up in Peterborough, Ontario. Belle was a throwback to an earlier, more sensible, time in Angus breeding. She was taller, had no trouble delivering her calves, and had enough milk left over for the family table. What she did not have was the bulging muscles or handsome heads of the Hereford or the haute Angus in fashion. She was number 88254 in the Canadian Aberdeen-Angus Herd Book and she would go on to produce over 450 descendants on the Gibbet Hill Farm. She had in her left ear a tattoo reading "AGJ-5A", the original one in her right ear having faded to nothing. Belle was born September 10, 1946, on W.F. James' Georgetown, Ontario, farm out of Eppie of Malden, by Witch Bandolier of Malden.

The Gibbet Hill herd did not sell well in the 1950s, so Bill was forced to change bull types and buy a few faddish females to keep the business going. He sagely kept the foundation females and rode the times until 1967, when they switched back to traditional bull types like Endmann, Wye, and Canadian. The pendulum of fashion had swung back to the taller type of Angus kept on the farm all along. Bill's vision for the American Angus had become the standard for the modern type that exists today. The two Gibbet Hill lines, the Belle family producing most of the females, and the Dido family producing many of the bulls, were both descended from the original 10 cows imported from Ontario. It was with a real sense of pride that Bill Conley told an *Angus Journal* writer in 1994, "Most of our pedigrees are entirely Gibbet Hill breeding on the female side. It is rare today to find a pedigree completely from one program. We have registered calves this year that were 12th generation of our own breeding."

The best bull of all, PS Sasquatch 904, was brought to Groton as a calf in 1979 and stood as a stud for Select Sires for 11 years. His influence was so great that as many as 104 of his daughters were in the herd at one time. Practically everything in the 1994 Gibbet Hill herd possessed his stamp on one side or the other.

Marion's favorite part of owning a purebred Angus herd was the record keeping. A potential buyer was given complete records and a detailed genealogy. Marion kept impeccable herd books, each entry written by hand. She could write up the lineage for all of her cattle for dozens of generations. Unfortunately, when the farm was sold, these amazing documents were burned at Mrs. Campbell's request.

In 1959, Conley adopted Angus Herd Improvement Records or AHIR, a scientific starting point for making real improvements to the breed. Later, they adopted an advertising slogan touting this early commitment to the scientific method: "We did performance when performance wasn't cool." When Bill and Marion started in the cattle business, artificial insemination (AI), now an industry standard, was not allowed in a purebred operation. This changed eventually to five AI service bulls per herd and by 1985 to unlimited semen transfer. AI widened the gap between herds produced for performance and those for the show ring. Bill had AHIR science backing his claim that Gibbet Hill calves were superior genetically for traits such as ease of calving, birth weight, and gains.

AI was an essential piece in the success of the farm. In 1985, 12 bulls were used in the AI program and while semen could not be shipped into the United States, it was legal for export. Imported genetic material could be obtained if it was shipped in from Canada but it was subject to a long quarantine. Bill and Marion hit the road traveling to every U.S. state, Australia, New Zealand, and South Africa promoting their liquid silver. Their live bulls were loaded up and shipped to places like Fort Worth and Denver, where ranchers could see for themselves what was being offered in each tiny frozen test tube.

In 1965, Bill was chosen as the beef ambassador on a United States Department of Agriculture sanctioned trip to the USSR, joining 19 other experts representing all aspects of U.S. agriculture. Khruschev had been trying to grow wheat but the Soviet program was failing miserably due to unfavorable growing conditions and a lack of real expertise. The American government seized the opportunity to put together a group of men who no one would ever suspect of spying. The aggies enjoyed unprecedented access to the country at a time when foreigners did not travel unattended. They were the first Americans to go to Kazakhstan and the Black Sea. The CIA were so pleased they met the fellas at the airport and whisked them away for an old-fashioned Washington debriefing session.

During the 60s and 70s, people in America ate a lot of beef and the New England Angus Association had 150 members, with over 10 small breeders in the Groton area alone. As their herd grew, Gibbet Hill Farm switched from small local sales to the regional consignment sales but Gibbet Hill beef could still be bought at the local supermarket. Four of the New England Association sales were held at the farm as well five Cow Power Sales. That changed in the 80s as Americans learned the dangers of a red meat diet. Soon white meat or no meat was in fashion and beef producers began to worry about the future.

The American Angus Association came up with an idea that helped to save the cattle business. In 1982 they funded a program founded in 1978 called Certified Angus Beef® or CAB. Bill Conley was elected to the Association's board of directors that same year and was soon board president, and worked long hours developing strategies for convincing breeders, packing plants, and beef buyers to support the innovative program. It was a tough sell. The board wrestled with the value of the program, especially when its price tag reached $250,000 annually. Then CAB was "clobbered" by the USDA and consumer advocates who through misinformation labeled it an "outright bogus con scheme." The confusion started when the agency learned that the requirement for a steak to receive the certified label was not what its name implied. The piece of meat did not actually have to come from a purebred Angus steer, just one that looked like an Angus.

But a steer that looks like an Angus is as good as a purebred Angus in all the ways that mattered. The CAB program had to prove to the USDA that even Angus quarter-breds are strongly Angus in character. The Aberdeen Angus, when crossed with just about any other breed of cattle, produces an offspring that closely resembles the Angus parent in most of the important taste traits. To be CAB, the animal had to have had a 51% black hide when it was alive and have eight other characteristics—ones so strict that 92% of all cattle slaughtered don't make the cut:

- Neck hump of less than 2 inches
- 'A' maturity (9—30 months)
- Medium to fine degree of marbling (prime and top 35% choice),
- Medium or better marbling texture
- USDA yield grade (YG) 3.9 or leaner
- Moderately thick or thicker muscling
- No capillary ruptures
- No dark-cutting characteristics

The specifications make for a mouth-watering dining experience and packers nowadays pay a premium on the average of $40 per head for CAB beef. Soon everyone was ordering Angus beef: supermarkets, chefs, and shoppers. Knock-off certifications popped up everywhere. There are currently 36 other branded Angus programs monitored by the USDA but only the Certified Angus Beef® program is endorsed by the American Angus Association. The CAB program licenses special distributors called "center-of-the-plate" who market the product by aging, cutting, wrapping, and personally delivering it to private clubs, restaurants, hotels, and other institutions.

Beginning in 1986, Gibbet Hill Farm threw an annual tasting party for Bostonians. Many breeders had no clue about the marketing side of the business and many distributors of beef products had never stepped foot on a farm. Seminars introduced attendees to artificial insemination, castration, and other farm practices, helping them to appreciate how wise they were to have chosen food service over animal science. Bill Conley would have a steer led into a ring and he would personally chalk exactly where the rump roast or filet was located on the breathing animal. Everyone had ample opportunity to talk shop and eat lots and lots of certified Angus steaks and burgers. The farm day event was soon co-sponsored by Dole and Bailey*, an old Boston firm. A food show was added allowing Dole & Bailey vendors to display their delectables to Boston chefs who were awarded professional points from the American Culinary Federation.

In 1995, Bill Conley was inducted into the Angus Heritage Foundation, for his immense contributions to the American Angus breed. He is enshrined on a plaque at the American Angus Association in St. Joseph, Missouri, just a few miles down the road from the Conley Angus Farm run by Bill's two sons Bill Jr. and Tim Conley. Many of the Conley cattle in Missouri are descended from Belle of Ontario and Groton.

The Danielsons Remove from Groton

Marion moved her elderly mother, Barbara Deering Danielson, to the Greenbriar nursing home in Miami where she died on Saturday November 27, 1982 at the age of 93. Barbara's philanthropic credentials were extensive. She had been on the board or served as trustee to the Boston Museum of Science, the Boston Museum of Fine Arts, Perkins School for the Blind in Watertown, MA, and the Nashoba Hospital in Ayer, which she and Richard had helped to

---

* Founded in 1868, Cyrus Dole and Frank Bailey, farmers from Vermont opened an artisan butcher stall inside Faneuil Hall. Their names are still visible high on columns in the historic farmer's market.

found. She was survived by her sons Richard Jr. who lived in Santa Barbara, and James Deering who lived in Florida.

Marion Campbell lived another 16 years serving on the boards of Groton School, the Providence Journal Company, the Boston Museum of Science, and the Nashoba Hospital. She had begun to develop her disjointed farmlands in Groton, something the town of Groton tried to prevent. Houses were built along Broadmeadow Road below the Five Oaks farm of Billy Wharton and on her hayfields just north of the town forest in West Groton, but she held onto Gibbet Hill.

When she died on November 24, 1998, in New York City, her Groton estate was managed by the Marion Campbell Trust. The trust passed to her sons, who had lives of their own in Portland and Denver and had no interest in the Groton legacy of their mother and grandparents. What the townspeople of Groton feared most came true—Gibbet Hill was put up for sale and by the year 2000, Modern Continental had an approved plan for 78 houses on the property.

In the final hours, Steven Webber, a Groton native, bought the 338-acre farm and the 188-acre Brooks Orchard east of the farm for $10 million and vowed to keep the farm intact. He was awarded a standing ovation from the world's toughest audience, the Groton Town Meeting. The Webbers also bought the cow herd and descendants of Belle can still be seen grazing on the hill. In 2004, Josh, Jed, and Kate Webber opened the Gibbet Hill Grill restaurant and a function hall in the remaining barns where Angus steaks are a speciality on the menu. Due to government regulations, they can not serve beef raised from their own herd.

In 2009, the family hired a farm manager and started planting two acres of crops including heirloom varieties. Tomatoes, summer squash, beets, cucumbers, green beans, and herbs make it into the recipes offered at the Grill. From their website: "Gibbet Hill Grill is at the forefront of the local food movement. We are one of the only restaurants in New England that has a produce farm on site, and our chef shapes the menu around what is seasonally available. Located on the 500-acre Gibbet Hill Farm in Groton, MA, guests can experience farm-to-fork dining while enjoying the beautiful landscape of Gibbet Hill."

The castle was cleaned up and a safety railing and public path installed. Steven Webber sold 80 acres in Half Moon Meadow to Daniel L. McElroy, and restored the farm, which now features Hereford and Holstein cows, chickens, fruit trees, and berries. He sells vegetables from a farm stand in the summers.

ABOVE: A Gibbet Hill purebred Angus bull, 2007 (Photo by the author, 2007)

BELOW: Marion Campbell and Bill Conley in 1995 (*Angus Journal*).

CHAPTER 11

THE END OF THE DREAM

GRAND PLANS

One summer Sunday in 1992, sometime between the hours of two and four, I climbed the stairs of the old Boutwell House on Main Street behind Isabel Beal, Groton Historical Society President—Issy was a tiny dynamo of a woman in her 70s with black chin-length hair and sensible shoes. I had worked with her, Mary Ripley, and Barbara Whitehill the first Tuesday of the month for several years cataloging Groton houses for the Massachusetts Historical Commission. I had never seen her in anything but an A-line skirt. Issy was feisty, witty, and Republican, and like most people in town, I loved her. However, she was not organized, at least in the strictest sense of the word. She knew where things were but no one else did.

That day was a real triumph for me. I had finally talked her into letting me see the blueprints for "Shawfieldmont" which she guarded like everything else under her care like a dog with a steak bone. This was the start of my efforts to uncover the real reason for the Bancroft's change of plans back in 1912, which had set Gibbet Hill on a new course for the rest of the century. We sat at a large wooden table in the musty book-lined room across the hall from where President Grant had slept. Issy reached down and produced two large sheets of vellum which she ceremoniously unrolled, eyeing me suspiciously as if I would snatch them from her grasp and run down the stairs and out the door. I couldn't believe my eyes. The plans were imposing. In blue and black ink was the General's dream of Shawfieldmont.

Eleanor Skinner

Eleanor Skinner had discovered the plans in her father's house as she was packing up to move to a smaller cape on Old Ayer Road. Eleanor and her brother Thomas had grown up in the house on Main Street next to Lawrence Academy. Her father, Lawrence Park had moved the house there in 1906 from its original location right on the busy road, leaving behind the carriage house. The house was now high on Powder House Hill and featured a sweeping front lawn. When her mother died, Eleanor and her husband George moved in and stayed until 1984 when her husband died and she could no longer justify such a large home. The gray clapboard cape was within sight of her father's house.

I visited Mrs. Skinner 10 years later and she served me tea on her back sun porch and I sat in an overstuffed chair as she elaborated on the connections between her family and the Bancrofts. Mrs. Skinner is a reserved woman of impeccable manners, her expensive furnishings comfortable, tasteful, and understated. General Bancroft's children and Lawrence Park's children were second cousins. They had spent many happy summer days together. Lawrence had been an attendant at Hugh's wedding and Hugh stood at the First Parish Church altar beside Lawrence when he married Maria Davis Motley in 1905. When invited to tea by Mrs. Maria Park, Mrs. Mary Bancroft always wore her French gloves.

Lawrence Park

Lawrence Park was the perfect choice as architect for the Shawfieldmont project. William Amos hired him to design a baronial estate on Gibbet Hill. Though he was a first cousin once removed, Lawrence Park's appointment in 1904 was not a case of nepotism. He had trained as an architect.

Lawrence, a contemporary of Hugh Bancroft at Harvard, was an indifferent student until he spent a year at the School of Drawing and Painting in the Museum of Fine Arts in Boston in 1896–97. Family legend tells of his love for art and architecture "almost from the cradle." Soon after learning to talk, he chastised his nurse for a lack of interest in a nearby building under construction. After serving as an apprentice draftsman in the offices of Shepley, Rutan, and Coolidge, in 1901 he opened up his own architectural firm, Park and Kendall, at 8 Beacon Street, Boston.

Lawrence moved back to Groton from Worcester and commuted to Boston each day on the train, riding alone in the smoking car establishing an aloof reputation. His society was enjoyed by a select few who were also members of the Pewter Mug Club—men like Fred Field Bullard the composer, Ralph Cram the architect, and publisher Herbert Copeland. Talent alone was not enough to make a firm successful, however, and he found the business side of things irksome. Without his commissions remodeling the First Parish Church in Groton and the plans for Shawfieldmont, his career as an architect would have been a complete failure.

By birth an erudite country squire, he established himself in life as a scholar of high degree. Art history rather than architecture was his true calling and in 1914 he found himself absorbed and productive. Like many gentlemen, he contributed to the perpetuity of his ancestors by writing a genealogy of the descendants of Major Thomas Savage for the New England Historical and Genealogical Register. While at this task he became fascinated with the Savage family paintings, stimulating a lifelong passion for colonial portraiture. With characteristic singleness of purpose, he began traveling constantly with a sketchbook and made detailed pencil copies of the portraits he studied.

Park's first attempt at scholarship involved the work of Joseph Badger. He established Badger as a major artist of colonial portraiture unmentioned up to that time in American art history texts. Previously, most of Badger's paintings had been attributed to the better known John Singleton Copley or Joseph Blackburn. Park's critical study was well received by the Massachusetts Historical Society and he published his catalog in 1918.

Charles Knowles Bolton, a trustee of the Massachusetts Historical Society, recalls a story of Park's artistic sleuthing. Park discreetly inquired about a certain portrait obtained from the estate of the late George F. Parkman. Charles recalled that the Society owned the painting but no one knew the name of the artist or the sitter. Lawrence offered Bolton $50 for the painting and after being refused admitted that "it was done by Mather Brown and represents the earliest known portrait of President John Adams."

Lawrence Park had an uncanny ability to discern the origins of a painting. His intuition was legendary. He once walked through a room at the Athenæum and announced, "There is a good portrait by John Johnson." When asked how he knew, Park replied "Oh, I don't know how I know, I just know." It was later discovered, after research at the Registry of Probate, the donor had mentioned the painting was by John Johnson.

This tall, unathletic, bespectacled man was an endearing character walking around Groton at the turn of the century. He served for a number of years on the board of the Lowthorpe School of Landscape Architecture and Horticulture for Women, located next door to him on Main Street. Founded by Mrs. Edward Gilchrist Low in 1901, Lowthorpe School was the first of its type for women. In an era when the only suitable vocation for middle-class women from good families was nurse or teacher, the school offered courses in engineering and botany. The Lowthorpe Georgian school house was located in the same building in which Margaret Fuller, as a girl, had attended Miss Prescott's School.

The trivial duties of daily life escaped Lawrence Park as he wandered through his apple orchards contemplating the beauty around him with pencil in hand. Without his inherited means, a hundred years earlier he might have ended up in the town poor farm, but he could live as he chose. He loved to sketch the designs on gravestones, many of which were carved by his ancient Groton ancestor William Park.* Another ancestor, Stuart James Park, had been a well-known contractor and builder, erecting massive granite public buildings. Lawrence Park's mother, Elizabeth, had been a Lawrence and a Bigelow, and his grandmother was the aunt of William Amos Bancroft.

---

*   Four generations of Park men carved slate headstones in Middlesex County. The first was William Park, who immigrated from Scotland to Boston in 1756. Most of their stones featured elaborate winged skulls and floral borders. The tall Park family stones in the Groton Old Burying Ground are undecorated.

Lawrence Park went on to write the definitive catalog on Joseph Blackburn, ensuring Blackburn had a good inch and a half on the bookshelf of American colonial art. However, Park is best remembered for his biography of Gilbert Stuart, completed as he struggled with very poor health. He died on Sunday morning, September 28, 1924, nearly 51 years of age. Two years later his *Gilbert Stuart; An Illustrated Descriptive List of His Works Compiled By Lawrence Park With an Account of His Life By John Hill Morgan and an Appreciation By Royal Cortissoz* was published in four volumes.

What Became of Shawfieldmont?

The plans before me at the Groton Historical Society reading room were on a large scale and, had they been completed, would have cost a fortune to build. The foundation alone was to have been 80 by 200 feet —16,000 square feet. The exterior walls and some of the interior walls, at two feet thick, would have been constructed of fieldstone. Each of the eight bedrooms on the second floor had its own fireplace, bath, and several closets. Almost all the ceilings were a full 16-feet high, (a ceiling is high at 9 or 10 feet high) making the space outrageously expensive to heat. There were 22 total rooms on the first and second floor with 13 fireplaces and 5 servants' quarters. There was probably also a third floor that had not yet been designed, or the plans may be lost. The plans imply that this floor would also have been livable space, as stairs ascending to it mirrored the grand staircase on the first floor, and perhaps it would have been the location of a ballroom or observatory for spectacular views of Mt. Wachusett.

The ground floor was designed to entertain on a scale suitable for a royal or presidential visit. The central drawing room was 49 by 32 feet and was flanked on either side by 32-foot square side drawing rooms providing a continuous entertaining space that could spill out onto two half-moon terraces with a spectacular view of Groton and the mountains beyond. Opposite the central drawing room was a 10-foot wide grand staircase ascending up to a landing then twisting to either side. North of the stairs was a music room and to the south, the kitchen and dining room. The entire northern end of the mansion housed the traditional paneled library. The architectural drawings indicated that east—west walls were to be taken up with gigantic fireplaces and the north end was to provide the perfect indirect lighting for snuggling up to the fire with a good book. A magnificent wall of glass stretched upward in four two-story sections each 16 feet wide. A gallery on the second floor, right off his bedroom, would have given the General access to a wonderful view of his farmlands and Martin's Pond. To complete his command post, Lawrence Park provided the General with an "armory" hidden under part of the main stairway. Shawfieldmont would have rivaled the great manor houses of England and Europe. As I looked at the plans, I had so many questions. Why had William Amos Bancroft abandoned his Groton estate?

It would take me over 10 years of dedicated research to answer this question to my satisfaction but the evidence remains indirect and circumstantial. Two explanations unravel from what I uncovered. Both are connected to the fact that the world changed at the turn of the century and the General could not. The failure to adapt is the beginning of extinction for any organism.

Evidence

I knew that the summer of 1912 had been horrendous for the Bancroft family. The General had been at the center of a violent strike that ended with his company accepting unionization. The Bancroft name had been in the papers on a daily basis. This might have been enough to deter any man from a major building project but somehow I had always doubted the strike was the full story. What I finally dug up was surprising.

General William Amos Bancroft, a man who appeared to be rational in every way, had lost a large portion of his fortune in a series of bad business deals aggravated by the economic decline of 1907. Mary Bancroft, the General's granddaughter, had left dozens of clues in a little novel titled *Upside Down in the Magnolia Tree* written in 1954. In the introduction she reveals, "General Dana is a portrait of my grandfather as I remember him." An illustration by Paul Galdone at the beginning of chapter seven is an exact replica of a postcard picturing the bungalow on Gibbet Hill. The names in the novel were changed (except Nolan) but many are easily recognizable, such as T.C. Bartlett for C.W. Barron. Mary strengthened the case in the first four chapters of her book *Autobiography of a Spy* published in 1983. From these two books and other corroborating sources, I pieced together a likely scenario of Bancroft's financial failure. It all began with Boston's speculation in copper mining.

Copper Rush

Copper was a very hot commodity in the late 1800s. Its use rose exponentially as the promise of yards of copper wires in every home across America rapidly became reality and speculators, like alchemists in the middle ages, envisioned turning copper into pure gold. Profits were staggering and investors were lining up to sink entire fortunes into the next mining venture. For a brief spell Boston was at the heart of all the action.

The shiny red metal is found everywhere on earth but in such small quantities that ore at just 5% copper content is considered a "bonanza." Incredibly rich veins range in grades of 40% to 50%. Three areas have most of the world's copper veins—Australia, Russia, and North America. Before the Industrial Revolution, most of the copper used in making American brass came from English mines in Cornwall and Devon. Early 1840 saw the rise of domestically mined copper from Michigan, although small amounts had been extracted since colonial times. In 1842, the US government had made a prudent purchase from the Chippewa Indians. The strip of land jutting into Lake Superior revealed rocks so pure in copper that barely any smelting would be needed to yield commercial grade metal. The subsequent Houghton report touched off the first real American mining rush, a few months before the more famous California Gold Rush. Like the California version, at the beginning of the copper rush men got rich by taking advantage of crude living conditions and nonexistent modes of transportation. They sold mining equipment, over-priced steaks, and ladies of the night. The Civil War and its demand for metals changed all that. Just about everyone in copper got rich.

Busy Victorian men were loath to keep all their wealth in banks. Panics came at regular intervals and a sudden run on a bank could cause it to fail in less than 24 hours, leaving the rest of the slower depositors bankrupt. Copper seemed like an easy and profitable way to invest piles of extra cash. In 1864, Edwin J. Hulbert and his brother laid claim to two exceptional mines which became the Calumet & Hecla Company.* Financed by Boston capital and led by Harvard-educated Quincy Adams Shaw, it thrived from 1867 to 1884 as the largest and richest copper mine in the world. Boston knew a good thing when it dug it up and Northern Michigan became a second Back Bay, with dozens of small mines traded on the Boston Stock Exchange making Boston second only to London in copper marketing.

Copper enterprises were just technical enough that investors took a hands-off approach, allowing the scientists to conduct most of the business. New mining companies were started by syndicates of wealthy friends of mine owners who placed them in the hands of capable managers and, in return, investors expected more than two-thirds of the mine's earnings in dividends. As a wasting asset,

---

*   Alexander Agassiz, son of famous Swiss naturalist and Harvard professor Louis Agassiz, took over as director of the mine in 1867. Alexander had an engineering degree and managed a coal mine after school yet was reluctant to take on this new job. It made him very rich. Shaw married Alexander's sister. Agassiz succeeded Shaw as titular head of the company, a position handed down to his son upon his death. In 1874 he also assumed his father's chair at Harvard.

it ran out over time—copper investing was only attractive if it paid out in dividends a portion of current earnings and original capital. No other business venture offered anything close to that rate of return on investment. Profits like these attracted an interesting group of characters.

Panic of 1907

The headline in the *Boston Post* of October 17, 1907 read:

COPPER BREAKS HEINZE—WATERLOO COMES TO YOUNG NAPOLEON AND BANKS TOTTER

Twenty-six years before the Federal Deposit Insurance Act came into being, and F. Augustus Heinze lost $50 million on October 14, 1907. Roller-coaster copper prices had plummeted from $62 to $15 and the market went crazy. In addition to being a copper speculator, Heinze was a newly minted bank owner with next to nothing in experience. He resigned his position as president of Mercantile National Bank after learning his Butte Montana Savings Bank had also failed. Depositors had caught wind of an attempt to corner the stock of United Copper Company. A run on the Mercantile Bank began the next day.

As the financial climate turned red, super hero J.P. Morgan stepped in to save the day, commenting that he simply "decided that the time had come for him to take action." He saved the day for the Trust Company of America but not for the Mercantile. Skittish depositors then began a run on Knickerbocker Trust Company when they learned its president Charles T. Barney was a pal of Heinze. Morgan refused to offer aid to Knickerbocker Trust because it was basically unsound. Rumors suggesting the Trust Company of America was entangled in Heinze's web of banks, brokerage houses and trust companies in New York were largely untrue, but shaky depositors would rather have a stuffed mattress. Out of $60 million in total deposits, Trust Company of America ended up paying out $47.5 million to customers over a span of two weeks.

J.P. Morgan talked bankers and the U.S. government into pouring over $50 million into ailing banks and the stock market to quell the bleeding—and he did it in just 15 minutes. John D. Rockefeller deposited $10 million of his own money into New York banks. Still the lines in front of the tellers remained blocks long. Morgan marched down to the New York Clearing House and "suggested" the bankers issue play money called "Clearing House Certificates." Banks substituted loan certificates for currency among themselves, allowing the real cash to flow to suitcases under beds. More than $500 million of the bank-to-bank IOUs ended up circulating. Morgan then "suggested" that all the New York ministers and priests give a rousing sermon on the virtues of American banking. It worked. The headlines soon giggled "Banks Leaving Trouble Behind."

Why Bancroft Lost Shawfieldmont

William Amos Bancroft was known to speculate. He was usually careful and conservative when it came to investments. He made it through the Panic of 1907 relatively unscathed, and he might have been feeling invulnerable. According to his granddaughter, he began to invest heavily in copper stocks in 1908. Copper mine stock prices had begun to rebound after their sharp drop in 1907 and the General fell prey to a stock promoter promising huge profits. Stocks that had been bought for $12 were selling for $70. Even at that price, Bostonians were buying anything with the name "consolidated copper" on the top of the certificate, forgetting the universal wisdom of buying low and selling high. William Amos sank a fortune into the volatile market.

The New York papers were filled with the woes of Wall Street. F.A. Heinze was indicted by the District Attorney on charges of misappropriating Mercantile Bank funds to bolster copper pool loans. He was convicted but his sentence was postponed so he could rat out all his "business associates". He seems to have been the victim of a gang of swindlers headed by Boston financier A.D.S. Adams and his partner D.S. Persch, who blamed the whole thing on Standard Oil men. Meanwhile copper companies were merging and producing, and then not producing, copper; prices held then dropped for a while, when claims dried up. It was a red metal mess and only the newspapers prospered.

I have been unable to uncover exactly who swindled William Amos Bancroft but there are many candidates. Granddaughter Mary Bancroft calls the promoter by the fictitious name "Jim Condon." After the second crash of copper stocks, Bancroft continued to make payments to "Jim Condon" to keep him out of jail, in the vain hope that he might recoup some of his money.

Jesse Lauriston Livermore is a strong possibility, gaining and losing several multi-million-dollar fortunes in his lifetime. He was born in South Acton and worked his way up in the newly formed Paine Webber Company but soon veered into swindles when he discovered the ease of trading stocks at glorified gambling dens called bucket shops. Livermore was to become the king of stock scams and questionable brokerage establishments. He did well in the Panic of 1907 and then blew nearly $3 million on a cotton trade. Many traders today worship Livermore and religiously read his biographies. He is blamed by some for the Crash of 1929, pocketing $100 million. The bumpy ride came to an end when he shot himself in 1940.

Another good candidate is Albert Smith Bigelow the first. Bert Bigelow was indeed an interesting man. He employed 10 servants to look after him in his old age at his exclusive residence on 30 Gloucester Street, Boston just off fashionable Comm Ave. He listed his occupation as mining company treasurer but at the time he was known in the papers as a "promoter". Bert wheeled and dealed mostly with copper stocks. Bigelow was also nearer to the type that might make Bancroft comfortable enough to open his wallet. From the same family as Bancroft's relative Timothy Bigelow, Bert attended the right clubs and knew the right people. His father Horatio had been one of the original investors in Calumet & Hecla started by Edwin J. Hulbert so copper was a family business. Bigelow also had a tobacco heiress for a wife which fits with a clue from *Upside Down in the Magnolia Tree*. He nearly ended up in jail when he tried to hide profits from a deal with Old Dominion Copper Mining and Smelting Company. The case went all the way to the Supreme Court in 1912. None other than Louis D. Brandeis argued it. Bigelow paid back $2.5 million, nearly a million more than the original amount awarded by the Massachusetts Supreme Court.

And then there was the particularly nasty tipster named George Graham Rice, born Jacob Simon Herzog. Most of the stocks Rice issued were fakes. He might just be the real "Jim Condon." Rice landed in jail in 1910 and then spent nearly $4 million trying to keep it from happening again. It didn't work. It is estimated he cheated the public out of $25 million. He wrote a book titled *My Adventures With Your Money* to pass the time in prison.

Whoever it was, the bottom line for General Bancroft was disaster and humiliation. He threw good after bad and never recouped his money. Mary Bancroft implied he kept his bad business deals hidden from his son Hugh for several years but eventually confided in him and they came to the conclusion that the only course of action was to sell Gibbet Hill. None of his children wanted the place. Guy lived in New York, Catherine in France, and Hugh was well established in Boston and Cohasset. Still, it was a bitter blow to the General, who loved the farm and no doubt found it very difficult to admit defeat. A week before the bungalow and all the land was sold to local speculators, he was in town trying to convince everyone he had decided not to sell after all. He was certainly not a poor man—his salary at the Boston Elevated Railway was the highest in the state—but he had nowhere near enough of his fortune left to keep such a large place going. He finally had to admit there was no chance of realizing his dream of a grand baronial mansion on the top of Gibbet Hill.

Sometime in the late 1950s or early 1960s, Bill Conley, manager of the Gibbet Hill Angus Farm was in his office next to Lowell Road. He saw a large gray Chevrolet pull into the driveway. Two older women got out of their car and looked up the hill toward the ruins of the castle. As Bill approached them, he noticed that they were both very tall. One of the women turned to him and commented, "I always wanted to see where Daddy spent all his money." The visitor was probably Catherine Bancroft Haviland. She had never seen her father's summer place, having lived in France and New York during the time it was being built. His dream now was just a pile of stones on Gibbet Hill, not even worth a hike up the hill for a closer look. Without introducing themselves the day-trippers got back in the two-toned Bel Air and drove away.

ABOVE: Bungalow ruin, 2007 (Photo by the author).

BELOW LEFT: Lawrence Park, portrait by Bachrach Studios, Boston.

BELOW RIGHT: Gravestone in the Groton Cemetery (Photo by the author).

From the Hills of "Shawfieldmont"

THERE, Wachusett and Watatick and the hill of English Joe,
Tall Monadnock, Peterboroughs, Uncanoonocks in a row;
Here, the valley of the Nashua, winding mirrored banks between,
And the wide and fertile meadows with their waving grasses green.

There the smoke of busy Fitchburg rises in the distant west,
And nearby the peaceful landscape smiles,— a dream of quiet rest;
Rounded hills and sloping pastures, here and there a farm-house white;
Babbling brooks and leafy woodlands, flowery fields in summer light.

Just beyond the elm-boughed village, over meadow broad and fair,
High above the halls of school-boys clustered near about it there,
Stands a tower of lofty beauty, and like sounds of foreign clime
From it come the notes of music, voices of the chapel chime.

To the east the spires of Westford shine across the forest trees,
North and south the towns and hamlets grateful feel New Hampshire's
    breeze.
Winding roads and sheen of lakelets, cattle browsing in the shade,—
All the land, with charms abundant, Nature's lavish hand has made.

Oft at morn the wondrous ghost lake comes like magic, with no sound,
Over fields and river valley, filling in the hills around;
And in birch canoes the red men glide in fancy down the stream,
Ere its mystic waters vanish with the great sun's dawning gleam.

Now the fleecy clouds resplendent float above the vale below,
Stately ships of heavenly grandeur from the seas of sunset glow;
Starry Night, with step reluctant, spreads her mantle over all,
While the moon her queenly crescent hides behind the mountain wall.

W. A. B.

Groton, Massachusetts, July, 1903.

ABOVE: From the 1903 pamphlet published by William Amos Bancroft (Library of Congress).

BIBLIOGRAPHY

Introduction

Beers, F.W., Louis E. Neumann, and Chas Hart. *County Atlas of Middlesex, Massachusetts*. (New York: J.W. Beers & Co., 1875).

Green, Samuel A. *The Boundary Lines of Old Groton*. (Groton, MA, 1885).

May, Virginia. *A Plantation called Petapawag: Some Notes on the History of Groton, Massachusetts*. (Groton: Groton Historical Society, 1976).

Take Note of Gibbet Hill

Avery, Ron. *Philadelphia Oddities*. Accessed April 2005: www.ushistory.org/oddities/gibbet.htm

Ellms, Charles. *The Pirates Own Book*. (Portland, ME: F. Blake, 1856).

Gibbet Hill. Accessed March 2003: www.mysteriousbritain.co.uk/england/cumbria

Held, Robert. *Inquisition*. (Florence, Italy: Qua D'Arno Publishers, 1985).

Hillman, Harold. "The Possible Pain Experienced During Execution By Different Methods," *Perceptions*, Vol. 22, 1993, 745–753, University of Surrey.

McGrory, David. *A History of Coventry*. (Chichester, England: Phillimore & Co., 2003).

Newman, Graeme. *Just and Painful*. (London: MacMillan Publishing, 1985).

Nutting, Rev. John Keep. *Nutting Genealogy: A Record of Some of the Descendants of John Nutting, of Groton, Mass*. (Syracuse, NY: C.W. Bardeen, 1908).

Plumridge, Andrew. *The Halifax Gibbet*. Accessed April 2003: www.metaphor.dk/guillotine/Pages/gibbet.html

Randa, Laura E., ed. *Society's Final Solution: A History and Discussion of the Death Penalty*. (Lanham, Maryland: University Press of America, 1997).

Groton Plantation

Barquet M.D., Nicolau, and Domingo M.D., Pere. "Smallpox: The Triumph over the Most Terrible of the Ministers of Death," *Annals of Internal Medicine*, 127, October 15, 1997, 625–642.

Bodge, George Madison. *Soldiers in King Philip's War*. (Baltimore: Genealogical Publishing Co., 1976).

Bradford, William. *Of Plimoth Plantation*. (New York: Knopf, 1976; Random House, 1981).

Butler, Caleb. *History of the Town of Groton*. (Boston, MA: Press of T.R. Marvin, 1848).

Callicott, J. Baird; Ybarra, Priscilla Solis. "The Puritan Origins of the American Wilderness Movement." Accessed April 2003: www.nhc.rtp.nc.us:8080/tserve/nattrans/ntwilderness/essays/puritan.htm

Connole, Dennis A. "Land occupied by the Nipmuck Indians of Central New England," *Bulletin of the MA Archaeological Society*, 38, October, 1976, 1–2.

Connole, Dennis A. *The Indians of the Nipmuck Country in Southern New England, 1630–1750: Historical Geography*. (Jefferson, NC: McFarland & Company, 2001): 225–226.

Doughton, Thomas L. *Unseen Neighbor: Native Americans of Central Massachusetts, A People Who Had "Vanished."* Accessed March 2003: www.geocities.com/quinnips/history/unseen.html

Gookin, Daniel. *Historical Collections of the Indians in New England*. (New York: Arno Press, 1972).

Green, Samuel Abbott. *Groton Historical Series*. (Cambridge, MA: University Press, 1877–1899).

Henderson, D.A. "Smallpox: Clinical and Epidemiologic Features," *Emerging Infectious Diseases*, Vol. 5, No. 4, July–August 1999, 537-539.

Johnson, Steven E. *Ninnuock (The People): The Algonkian People of New England*. (Marlborough, MA: Bliss Publishing Company, 1995).

Morton, Thomas. *New English Canaan*. (New York: Burt Franklin, 1967).

Scozzari, Lois. "The Significance of Wampum to Seventeenth Century Indians in New England." Accessed March 2003: www.hartford-hwp.com/archives/41/037.html

Sears, Clara Endicott. *The Great Powwow; The Story of the Nashaway Valley in King Philip's War*. (Boston: Houghton Mifflin Co., 1934).

Sultzman, Lee. "Compact Histories of First Nations." Accessed March 2003: www.tolatsga.org/compacts.html

Swanton, John R. "The Indian Tribes of North America," *Bureau of American Ethnology Bulletin*, 145, 1953, 17–27.

Thatcher, Oliver J. *The Library of Original Sources*. (Milwaukee: University Research Extension Co., 1907): 360–377.

Turner, Frederick Jackson. *The Frontier In American History*. (New York: Henry Holt and Co., 1921): Chapters 1 & 2.

Winthrop, John. *Reasons for the Plantation in New England*. Accessed April 2003: www.winthropsociety.org/reasons.htm

The Bancrofts of Groton

"Alumni Notes," *The Tech* (MIT), 21:3, October 24, 1901, 30.

Bodge, George Madison. *Soldiers in King Philip's War*. (Baltimore: Genealogical Publishing Co., 1976).

Butler, Caleb. *History of the Town of Groton*. (Boston, MA: Press of T.R. Marvin, 1848).

Dow, Joseph. *History of the Town of Hampton, New Hampshire*, Vol. 1. (Salem, MA: The Salem Publishing and Printing Co., 1893).

Eliot, Samuel Atkins. *A History of Cambridge (1630–1913)*. (Cambridge, MA: *The Cambridge Tribune*, 1913).

Frank, Douglas Alan. *The History of Lawrence Academy at Groton 1792 to 1992*. (Groton, MA: Lawrence Academy, 1992).

"Gen. Bancroft When He Was Known As 'Foxy'," *Boston Journal*, June 26, 1905.

Green, Samuel Abbott. *Facts Relating to the History of Groton, Massachusetts*, Vol II. (Cambridge, MA: University Press, 1914).

"Hon. William Amos Bancroft," *Biographical Review*, Vol. 27. (Boston, MA: Biographical Review Publishing Co., 1898).

Hurd, Duane Hamilton, ed. *History of Middlesex County, Massachusetts*, Vol. 1. (Philadelphia, PA: J.W. Lewis & Co., 1890).

May, Virginia. *Groton Houses: Some Notes on the History of Old Homesteads in Groton, Massachusetts.* (Groton, MA: Groton Historical Society, 1978).

Mumford, George Saltonstall. *Twenty Harvard Crews.* (Cambridge, MA: Harvard University Press, 1923).

New York Times, 1887: February 11, 1; February 22, 1; March 10, 5.

New York Times, 1910: January 21, 10.

Parks, Frank Sylvester, ed. *Genealogy of the Parke Families of Massachusetts.* (Washington, (Washington, DC: Henry A. Parks, 1909): 194–203.

Richards, William, and Thayer, William Roscoe. *The Harvard Graduates' Magazine,* Vol. XXX. (Boston: The Harvard Graduates' Magazine Association, 1921–1922).

The Essex Antiquarian, 1:1, 1897, 10–14. (Salem, MA).

Shawfieldmont

Bancroft, Mary. *Upside Down In the Magnolia Tree.* (Boston, MA: Little, Brown, and Company, 1952).

Bancroft, Mary. *Autobiography of a Spy.* (New York: William Morrow and Company, 1983).

Clarke, Bradley H. *The Boston Transit Album.* (Cambridge, MA: Boston Street Railway Association, 1977).

"Groton Hunt Club Finds New Quarters Atop Gibbet Hill," *Boston Evening Transcript,* August 1, 1931, magazine section, 1.

"History of the Groton Water Company." Accessed October 2022: www.grotonwater.org/history

Kruh, David. *Always Something Doing: Boston's Infamous Scollay Square.* (New York: Faber and Faber, 1990).

Lethaby, W.A. "Art is Thoughtful Workmanship," *The Imprint.* (London, January 1913).

Quinquennial Catalogue of Harvard. 1636–1930. (Cambridge, MA: Harvard University Press, 1930).

"Richard Morris Hunt, American Architect," *Britannica Online Encyclopædia*. Accessed December 2009: www.britannica.com/EBchecked/topic/276963/Richard-Morris-Hunt

Sullivan, Mark. *Our Times: The United States 1900–1925*. Vol. 1–4. (New York: Charles Scribner & Sons, 1930).

The Equestrian Statue of Major General Joseph Hooker: Erected and Dedicated by the Commonwealth of Massachusetts. (Boston: Wright & Potter Printing Company, 1903).

Wilde, Oscar. "Art and The Handicraftsman," *Essays and Lectures by Oscar Wilde*. (London: Methuen and Co., 1908).

The End of the Line

"Bancroft Sells Home in Country," *Boston Journal*, October 15, 1912, 3.

"Boston Railroad Strikes," *The New York Times*, February 11, 1887, 1.

"Boston Strike Ends," *The Motorman and Conductor*, 20:9, August 1912, 6-8.

"BOSTON STRIKERS WIN.; Conductors and Motormen Victorious in a 53-Day Struggle." *The New York Times*, July 30, 1912, 6.

"Cambridge Strikers Defeated," *The New York Times*, March 10, 1887, 5.

"Car Men Tell of Grievance," *Boston Journal*, June 28, 1912, 7.

"Claim Dynamite Plot to Blow up Reservoir at Chestnut Hill," *Boston Journal*, June 11, 1912, 1.

Clarke, Bradley H. *The Boston Transit Album*. (Cambridge, MA: Boston Street Railway Association, 1977).

"Differences Bar Ending of Strike," *Boston Herald*, July 26, 1912, 1.

Fifteenth Annual Report of the Directors of the Boston Elevated Railway Co. (Boston, MA: Press of Geo. H. Ellis Co., 1912).

"History." Boston Carman's Union, local 589. Accessed December 2012: https://carmensunion589.org/about-us/3774-2

"L Appeals to Public," *Boston Herald*, June 8, 1912, 3.

"Motorman Saved from Lynch Mob," *Boston Journal*, July 10, 1912, 1.

"Punish Guilty, Says Governor," *Boston Herald*, June 23, 1912, 3.

Shattuck papers. Vol. 21. Massachusetts Historical Society. Boston, MA. "State Board Condemns Elevated; Bancroft Summoned by Grand Jury," *Boston Journal*, July 23, 1912, 1.

"Strike Endorsed by Labor Unions," *Boston Journal*, June 10, 1912, 4.

"Strikers Hold Great Parade," *Boston Herald*, June 12, 1912, 5.

"The Confession and Dying Words of Samuel Frost, Who is to be Executed this Day, October 31, 1793, for the Horrid Crime of Murder." Accessed October 30, 2022: https://bostonraremaps.com/wp-content/uploads/2022/01/BRM4063-Confessions-Samuel-Frost-1793_lowres-scaled.jpg

"The Hoodlums Aroused," *The New York Times*, February 22, 1887, 1.

Dr. Ayres' Hospital

"A History of Veterans Healthcare." Accessed June 2005: www.va.gov/facmgt/medical-care.asp

Bureau of Veteran Reestablishment. Hearing Before the Committee on Interstate and Foreign Commerce of the House of Representatives, Sixty-sixth Congress, Third Session on H. R. 14961, January 7, 1921 (Washington Government Printing Office, 1921).

Caldwell, Mark. *The Last Crusade: The War on Consumption 1862–1954*. (New York: Atheneum, 1988).

"Chain of Hospitals for Disabled Men," *New York Times*, April 6, 1919, 9.

"Colonel Forbes Under Fire," *The Outlook*, November 1923, 477–478.

"Department of Veterans Affairs (VA), a Brief History." Accessed June 2005: www.va.gov.vafhis.htm

"Gross Neglect and Profiteering in Caring for Disabled Veterans," *The Literary Digest*, February 4, 1922, 46.

Hakim, Joy. *War, Peace, and All That Jazz*. (New York: Oxford University Press, 1995).

Kolata, Gina Bari. *Flu: The Story of the Great Influenza Pandemic of 1918 and the Search for the Virus That Caused It*. (New York: Farrar, Straus and Girous, 1999).

Murphy, J. Prentice. "Meeting the Scourge: How Massachusetts Organized to Fight Influenza Told for the Benefit of Other States," *The Survey*, October 26, 1918.

Ott, Katherine. *Fevered Lives: Tuberculosis in the American Culture Since 1870.* (Cambridge, MA: Harvard University Press, 1996).

"National Home for Disabled Volunteer Soldiers." Accessed June 2005: www.va.gov/facmgt/NHDVS.asp

"Parents Ask Legion to Block Plan to Transfer Wounded," *Boston Herald*, July 29, 1920.

Price, M.D., George M. "Disabled in the Line of Duty: The Problem of the Tuberculous Soldier," *The Survey*, March 22, 1919, 889–890.

Sawyer, Helen McCarthy. *People and Places of Groton.* (Littleton, NH: Sherwin/Dodge, 1986).

Sawyer, Helen McCarthy. *More People and Places of Groton.* (Littleton, NH: Sherwin/Dodge Publishing, 1987).

"Sprague Calls For Hospital Inquiry," *New York Times*, August 7, 1922, 8.

"The Conviction of Colonel Forbes," *The Literary Digest*, February 14, 1925, 11.

"The Indictment of Forbes," *The Outlook*, March 12, 1924, 413–414.

"The Veterans' Bureau Called Wasteful and Inefficient," *The Literary Digest*, April 14, 1923, 67–71.

Burning Cross

Review, January 22, 1927.

Dirks, Tom. *Top 100: Birth of a Nation.* Accessed February 27, 2005: www.filmsite.org/birt.html

Evans, Hiram Wesley. "The Klan's Fight for Americanism," *North American Review*, Vol. 223, March, 1926, 33–63.

"Groton Church Lightless," *New York Times*, July 9, 1926, 33.

Ingalls, Robert P. *Hoods: The Story of the Ku Klux Klan.* (New York: G.P. Putnam's Sons, 1979).

Jackson, Kenneth T. *The Ku Klux Klan In The City*. (New York: Oxford University Press, 1967).

Myers, William Starr. "Know Nothing and the Ku Klux Klan," *North American Review*, Vol. 219, January, 1924, 1–7.

"Negros Mob Photo Play," *New York Times*, April 18, 1915, 15.

"The Klan Walks In Washington," *Literary Digest*, Vol. 86, August 22, 1925, 7–8.

Wolkovich-Valkavicius, William. *Immigrants and Yankees*. (W. Groton, MA: William Wolkovich-Valkavicius, publisher, 1981).

Wolkovich-Valkavicius, William. "The Ku Klux Klan In The Nashoba Valley," *Historical Journal of Massachusetts*, Winter 1990, 61–80.

Mr. Danielson Comes to Groton

Albright, Alan. *American Volunteers at the Beginning of the War*. (Blérancourt Exhibition Catalog, 1993).

Ashburn, Frank D. *Peabody of Groton: A Portrait*. (Cambridge, MA: The Riverside Press, 1967).

Assad, Matt; Frassinelli, Mike; Venditta, David; Whelan, Frank. "Forging America: The Story of Bethlehem Steel," *Allentown Morning Call*, December 14, 1913, special section.

"Charles G. Dawes Biography." Nobel Museum website. Accessed April 2005: www.nobel.se/peace/laureates/1925/dawes-bio.html

"Charles Deering," *The National Encyclopedia of American Biography*, Vol. 33. (New York: James T. White and Company, 1947).

"Charles Deering Estate." Accessed June 23, 2005: www.co.miami-dade.fl.us/parks/Parks/deering.htm

Chuppa-Cornell, Kimberly. "The U.S. Women's Motor Corps in France, 1914–1921," *Historian*, June 22, 1995.

Drake, Barbara. "The Deering Estate at Cutler," *Florida History and the Arts*, Vol. 8, 5, 2000.

Folsum, Merrill. *Great American Mansions And Their Stories*. (New York: Hastings House Publishers, 1963).

Hansen, Arlen J. *Gentlemen Volunteers: The Story of the American Ambulance Drivers in the Great War, August 1914–September 1918.* (New York: Arcade Publishing, 1996).

"Hemingway an Ambulance Driver – ARC Section Four. 1918." Accessed June 2005: www.ernest.hemingway.com/ambulancedriver.htm

"James Deering," *The National Encyclopedia of American Biography*, Vol. 20. (New York: James T. White and Company, 1929).

Kintrea, Frank. "Old Peabo and the School," *American Heritage Magazine*, Vol. 21, 6, October/November 1980.

Lundberg, Ferdinand. *The Rich and the Super Rich*. (New York: Lyle Stuart, 1968).

"Married In Paris After Troth Denied," *New York Times*, July 7, 1914.

Mata, Jose F. "Defense of the Hemisphere: An Historical Postscript," *Joint Force Quarterly*, 11, Spring 1996, 73–75.

"McCormick History." Accessed November 2004: www.mccormick-intl.com/en/history/mccormick/default2.htm

Olson, Stanley. *John Singer Sargent: His Portrait*. (New York: St. Martin's Press, 1986).

Ruggenberg, Rob. "What did Daddy do in the Great War?" Accessed March 2003: www.geocities.com/~worldwar1/famouspeople.html

Shand-Tucci, Douglass. *The Art of Scandal: The Life and Times of Isabella Stewart Gardner*. (New York, NY: HarperCollins Publishers, 1997).

Tully, Thomas A., Editor. *History of the Class of 1907* Yale College, Vol. II. (New Haven, CT: Yale University, 1907).

Wilson, Mark R. "International Harvester Company," *Encyclopedia of Chicago*. Accessed March 2007: www.encyclopedia.chicagohistory.org/pages/2723.html

The Groton Hunt

"Arnold Arboretum, Harvard University," *Bulletin of Popular Information*, Series 3, Vol. V September 21, 1931, No. 14 & 15.

Danielson, Richard E. *Martha Doyle and Other Sporting Stories*. (New York: The Derrydale Press, 1938).

"Debs," *Time Magazine*, October 22, 1941.

Floyd, Margaret Henderson. "Sturgis, John Hubbard," *American National Biography.* (New York: Oxford University Press, 1999). Accessed January 7, 2009: www.libarts.ucok.edu/history/faculty/ roberson/course/1493/supplements/chp19/19.%20John%20 Hubbard%20Sturgis.htm

"Groton Hunt Club Finds New Quarters Atop Gibbet Hill," *Boston Evening Transcript*, August 1, 1931, magazine section, 1.

Kenison, Arthur M. *Frederic C. Dumaine.* (Manchester, NH: Saint Anselm Press, 2000).

Lawrence, Robert M. *Historical Sketches of Some Members of the Lawrence Family.* (Boston, MA: Rand Avery Company, Printers, 1888).

Lowell, Thomas. *Pageant of Life.* (New York: P.F. Collier & Sons Corp., 1941).

"Lowthorpe Plans 40th Anniversary," *New York Times*, August 25, 1940.

Mason, Walter Esplin. *Dogs of All Nations.* (England: S.l.: s.n., 1915). DOI: https://doi.org/10.5962/bhl.title.31578

"North Hill Hunt." Accessed March 2004: http://members.cox.net/ northhillshunt/index.htm

"Raid on the New Haven," *Time Magazine*, May 17, 1948.

Sawyer, Helen McCarthy. *People and Places of Groton.* (Littleton, NH: Sherwin/Dodge, 1986).

Watson, J.N.P. *The Book of Foxhunting.* (New York: Arco Publishing Company, 1978).

Nothing But Black Cows

Arnold, Alison. "Social Chatter," *Boston Herald*, December 22, 1949.

"Breed of Livestock—Angus Cattle." Accessed November 2005: www. ansi.ok.state.edu/breeds/cattle/angus, Oklahoma State University.

"Campbell, Douglass," *New York Times*, March 30, 200, C-13.

Carlson, Laurie Winn. *Cattle: An Informal Social History*. (Chicago: Ivan R. Dee, 2001).

Chivers, C.J. "Marion D. Campbell, 77, Atlantic Monthly Editor, Former Journal Director," *Providence Journal*, November 25, 1998: C-06.

Cotton, Jim, ed. "Weighing Those Hard Choices: A Familiar Role For Bill Conley," *Angus Journal*, November 1985, 34, 35.

"Danielson's Daughter to Head Atlantic," *Boston Herald*, September 1957.

Doherty, William, and Fitzgerald, Joan. "Former Owners of Atlantic Sue Zuckerman," *Boston Globe*, June 11, 1981, economy section.

Fenton, John H. "Weeks Retires as Atlantic's Editor-in-Chief After 28 Years; Manning Succeeds Him," *New York Times*, January 24, 1966, 22.

Fitzgerald, Joan. "Ex-Owner Offers To Take Back Atlantic Monthly," *Boston Globe*, June 27, 1981, economy section.

Franklin, Lori. "From Downtown to Down On The Farm," *Angus Journal*, June–July 1994, 216, 221.

Husseini, Sam, and Naureckas, Jim. "Zuckerman Unbounded: A Developer/Publisher Brings His Influence to the Daily News," *Extra!* January/February, 1993.

"Joan Davisson Bows at Dance," *New York Times*, June 25, 1939, D3.

Knight, Michael. "Atlantic Monthly to Be Sold to Developer," *New York Times*, March 1, 1980, 1.

Mayer, Janet. "New England Endeavor," *Angus Journal*, June–July 1994, 222–224.

McKibben, Gordon. "Zuckerman Testifies of Deception," *Boston Globe*, May 15, 1987, 67.

McKibben, Gordon. "Old Memos Led Zuckerman To Halt Payments," *Boston Globe*, May 16, 1987, 35.

McKibben, Gordon. "Atlantic Monthly Trial Opens," *Boston Globe*, May 17, 1987, 61.

Mehegan, David. "Federal Judge Upholds Verdict In Atlantic Case," *Boston Globe*, December 1, 1987, 67.

Montgomery, M.R. *A Cow's Life: The Surprising History of Cattle and How the Black Angus Came to Be Home on the Range.* (New York: Walker & Company, 2004).

"More About Matt." Vassar. Accessed November 2005: http://collegerelations.vassar.edu/matthew.html

"Mortimer Benjamin Zuckerman. The 400 Richest Americans," *Forbes.* Accessed February 2006: www.forbes.com/lists/2005/54/W07H.html

Murphy, Cullen. "A History of The Atlantic Monthly," *The Atlantic Online.* Accessed September 9, 2005: www.theatlantic.com/about/atlhistf.htm

"Real Estate Developer to Buy Atlantic Monthly," *Chicago Sun-Times,* March 1, 1980.

"Seven Who Made a Difference Slated for Induction Into Angus Heritage Foundation," *Angus Journal,* November 1995, 62, 63.

"The 400 Richest Americans," *Forbes.* Accessed February 2006: www.forbes.com/lists/2005/54/Rank_1.html

"The History and Development of the World's Finest Beef Breed." Accessed November 2005: www.aberdeen-angus.com/history.html

Wolff, Michael. "This Media Life: The Me in Media," *New York Magazine,* December 7, 1998.

The End of a Dream

Bolton, Charles Knowles. *Lawrence Park.* (Boston, MA: Massachusetts Historical Society Proceedings, 1924).

Gormley, Myra Vanderpool. "Gravestone Chronicles: Art, History, and Genealogy." Accessed March 19, 2007: www.ancestry.com/columns/myra/Shaking_Family_Tree10-09-97.htm

Hartford, Norm. "Discovering the Lost Castle," *Groton Herald,* April 24, 1985.

Keys, C.M. "The Get-Rich-Quick Game," *The Worlds' Work,* March 1911, 14112–14121. Accessed March 2007: http://earlyradiohistory.us/1911rich.htm

Lowthorpe School of Landscape Architecture and Horticulture for Women (catalog) 1910–1917. Accessed April 2007:

http://ocp.hul.harvard.edu/ww/outsidelink.html/http://nrs.harvard.edu/urn-3:FHCL:441029.

"Mines, Metals, Medals," *Time Magazine*, March 4, 1935. Accessed March 2007: www.time.com/time/magazine/article/0,9171,931543,00.html

Moen, Jon. "Panic of 1907," EH.Net Encyclopedia, edited by Robert Whaples. Accessed March 2007: http://eh.net/encyclopedia/article/moen.panic.1907

Navin, Thomas R. *Copper Mining & Management*. (Tucson, AR: University of Arizona Press, 1978).

"Panic of 1907." Federal Reserve Bank of Boston website. Accessed March 2007: www.bos.frb.org/about/pubs/panicof1.pdf

"Rice Resumes," *Time Magazine*, January 29, 1934. Accessed March 2007: www.time.com/time/magazine/article/0,9171,787802,00.html

Rickard, Thomas Arthur. *The Copper Mines of Lake Superior*. (New York: *The Engineering and Mining Journal*, 1905).

Interviews Conducted by the Author

Beal, Isabel. November 9, 1990.
Brown, Douglas. April 1, 2004, March 31, 2005.
Conley, William. November 22 and 25, 2002.
Duke, Winn. March 28, 2005.
Elletherio, Zoe. March 28, 2005.
Fitch, Harlan. October 24, 2003.
Franzek, John. December 2, 2002.
Locke, Debbie. October 2002.
Mountain, Benjamin. 1990.
Naylor, Louise. January 2003.
Norstrum, Dick. April 24, 2002.
Prouty, Roger. March 30, 2005.
Robbins, Ollie Tolles. October 8, 2002.
Skinner, Eleanor. 1994.
Tolles, Ramona. March 25, 2005.
Webber, Steven. February 6, 2004.

INDEX